English Pronunciation:

Pronounce It Perfectly in 4 Months
Fun & Easy

Fluent English Publishing

Xiao, Ken
> English Pronunciation: Pronounce It Perfectly in 4 Months Fun & Easy

Copyright © 2018 by Ken Xiao

ISBN-13: 978-0-9981632-9-1   9|20
ISBN-10: 0-9981632-9-5

***** Audio available for purchase *****
Go to Amazon.com or
FluentEnglishPublishing.com

Listen to this often. Absorb the energy every time!

In a poor farming village, a child was born. In his childhood life, he was hungry. So hungry that even after over 30 years, he still remembers the hunger he'd been through in vivid details. There was no running water, so he had to carry water home using two buckets from a well that was half of a kilometer away. He was seven years old. The buckets of water were so heavy that he felt like two mountains on him. At the age of seven, he started to work in the fields to plant, cultivate, and harvest crops. At the age of seven, he started to collect firewood for cooking. At the age of seven, he started to cook for the entire family using an open fire. There was no electric stove, and he was lucky if he got electricity for lighting once a week. He started elementary school at the age of eight and dropped out of middle school at the age of 13.

He didn't speak any English when he moved to the United States at the age of 17. He started to learn English in ESL classes, and three years later, he was able to speak some broken English. Then he looked for the key to English fluency and found the secret. Following the secret for six months, he began to speak English like a native speaker.

He graduated high school, graduated college, and graduated graduate school.

Here is the best part: This country boy, this middle school dropout, who started at 20, for six months, who successfully learned to speak English like a native speaker, has no special talent! He's just an average boy you and I would see in the countryside. He's just an average man you and I would meet on the streets. All he did was following the secret, a secret that you'll learn in this book.

This country boy is talking right in front of you. This middle school dropout is me.

To your success,

Ken Xiao

About the Author

Ken Xiao

Ken is an English teacher who has walked in your shoes. He didn't speak any English when he moved to United States at the age of 17. After three years from speaking no English to speaking broken English, Ken looked for the key to English fluency and found the secret to success. Using that secret, Ken quickly learned to speak English like a native speaker in six months.

Ken has a bachelor's degree in Information Technology and a master's degree in Space Studies. He had been an interpreter with the United States Department of Defense. He's the creator of My Fluent English Formula which he used to help him speak English and two other languages like a native speaker. The secret in this book.

Ken is now an English teacher, school principal, and author.

Contents

Listen to this often. Absorb the energy every time!........................iv
About the Author...vi
Chapter 1: Take the Crab to the Beach...1
Chapter 2: Pronounce Perfectly, Fun & Easy!...............................4
Chapter 3: Vowel Overview...8
Chapter 4: The E sound..9
Chapter 5: The Slightly Different IH Sound.................................13
Chapter 6: The Easy EH Sound..19
Chapter 7: The Stronger /æ/ Sound..21
Chapter 8: The AH Sound...27
Chapter 9: The Similar UH Sound...30
Chapter 10: The AW Sound...34
Chapter 11: The OH Sound..36
Chapter 12: The Pay-Attention /ʊ/ Sound....................................40
Chapter 13: The Common OO Sound..43
Chapter 14: The Easy A Sound..47
Chapter 15: The I Sound...51
Chapter 16: The OW Sound...56
Chapter 17: The OY Sound..59
Chapter 18: The /ER/ Sound...61
Chapter 19: The Dropped Vowel Sounds......................................63
Chapter 20: The Reduced Vowel Sounds......................................64
Chapter 21: The Regular Vowel Sounds.......................................66
Chapter 22: The Stressed Vowel Sounds......................................67
Chapter 23: Intonation...69
Chapter 24: Consonant Overview..78
Chapter 25: The B, /B/ and the P, /P/ Sounds.............................80
Chapter 26: The D, /D/ and the T, /T/ Sounds............................89
Chapter 27: The F, /F/, the V, /V/, and the W, /W/ Sounds..........101
Chapter 28: The G, /G/ and the K, /K/ Sounds...........................111
Chapter 29: The H, /H/ Sound...119
Chapter 30: The L, /L/ and the R, /R/ Sounds............................121
Chapter 31: The M, /M/, N, /N/, and NG, /ŋ/ Sounds.................128
Chapter 32: The S, /S/ and the Z, /Z/ Sounds............................135
Chapter 33: The /Y/ Sound..142
Chapter 34: The /CH/ and the /J/ Sounds..................................144

Chapter 35: The /SH/ and the /ZH/ Sounds..................................149
Chapter 36: The TH Sounds...155
Chapter 37: The Roll Back Consonants.......................................164
Chapter 38: The Dropped Consonants..167
Chapter 39: The Missing Consonants...169
Chapter 40: Liaison...170
Chapter 41: To Our Journey!...179

Chapter 1: Take the Crab to the Beach

You want to learn English pronunciation but there are so many books to choose from. You don't know which book is right for you, and you don't know which book can give you the results you want.

Now look at this:

My name is Ken Xiao. I didn't speak any English when I moved to the United States at the age of 17, but listen to my English now! The audio of this book is my voice!

In this book, you'll learn English pronunciation from a successful English teacher, me, who has walked in your shoes before. You'll learn to pronounce it perfectly in four months with 100% accuracy like me!

Take a look at the following pairs of words. Do they sound the same or different?
- Sheep, ship
- cop, cup
- food, foot

Yes, they sound different. How about these pairs?
- cap, cab
- life, live
- latter, ladder

Yes, they sound different, too. Look at the following sentences. Can you say them right?
- Walk up a hill in high heels to see how you'll feel.
- Friend A, "A friend in need is a friend indeed."
- Friend B, "Agreed! Give me your money."

How about these sentences. Can you say them correctly?
- Wipe a viper with a wiper is wise only if you're truly prepared to die.
- Wear your best vest facing west then give your kid this kit.
- Excuse me. what's your excuse to take back your bag?

If you think you've got them right, congratulations, you've got them wrong.

I have been in your shoes before, and I know you've got them wrong.

Many words in English sound so similar, too similar that we think they're the same. Pronouncing the right words wrong can meaning something else. Even slightly mispronouncing some words can damage everything.

Let's take a look at this sentence:

Take the crab to the beach.

That's what we intended to say, but you said it wrong. You mispronounced two words, embarrassed yourself, and ruined everything.

Do you know what you've pronounced wrong?

Let's train our ears to hear the slight differences between similar sounds and train our mouth to pronounce the slight differences between similar sounds.

For beginners, let's learn English pronunciation perfectly right away from the beginning.

For intermediate learners, let's correct our pronunciation and then perfect it.

For advanced learners, let's find out what we've got wrong, and then get them right.

For all learners, let's do so even if we have a tight schedule.

In this book, you will:
1. Learn English pronunciation.
2. Perfect your English pronunciation.
3. Do so easily.
4. Laugh.

Learn English pronunciation from the successful! Follow my steps in this book to learn English pronunciation and pronounce it perfectly with 100% accuracy! Let's achieve that in four months and have fun.

Chapter 2: Pronounce Perfectly, Fun & Easy!

In this book, we'll use an easy method to learn pronunciation and then perfect our pronunciation. Simply follow the instructions in this chapter to practice our pronunciation chapter by chapter.

In the book, we'll see instructions on lip positions and tongue positions. These are for our references only. Our lips and tongue will go automatic once we've mastered our pronunciation.

Here is one tip that works very well to perfect our pronunciation on any word – **pronounce it from the back.**

Let's take the word extraordinary for example. If we can't say it right, say it like this:

- Ry
- Nary
- Dinary
- Ordinary
- Raordinary
- Traordinary
- Extraordinary

This is extremely helpful to pronounce difficult words. In addition, let's look at the following two words.

Chain, Train

These two words sound similar or the same to many of us. However, we can clearly tell the differences and easily pronounce the differences. We'll learn this in details in the later chapters.

How do we perfect our pronunciation?

Practice!

Do you drive? Do you take the bus? The train? Do you walk? Do you work out? Do you cook? Do you wait in line for anything? Do you have any moment where your body is busy but your mind is free?

Any of these moments is a great moment to master our English pronunciation! This is how I got me to speak like a native speaker!

Even if a moment is just 60 seconds, put on our headphones and practice.

Now follow these steps to get our guaranteed remarkable results!

Step 1: Listen and Repeat At the Same Time
Listen to the audio of a chapter and repeat what you hear immediately. Do not wait until the end. Repeat immediately. It's OK to miss something the first few times. Just keep going without stopping.

Step 2: Finish Repeating the Whole Chapter
Listen to and repeat the chapter from the beginning to the end.

Step 3: Record Your Voice
Record your voice repeating the chapter. This is important. Do *not* skip it.

Find a recorder such as your computer, a cell phone or an MP3 recorder. Put on a pair of headphones and record your voice repeating the chapter from the beginning to the end.

Save the file and move on to Step 4.

Step 4: Finish Repeating the Chapter One More Time
Listen and repeat the chapter again from the beginning to the end.

Step 5: Immediately Go Back and Repeat the Words You Can't Say For As Many Times As You Need
Repeat the chapter again. This time, if there are words you can't say correctly, immediately stop and go back to them. Listen again and repeat. Try once, twice, three times, or more. Try as many times as you need until you can say all words correctly.

Step 6: Finish Repeating the Chapter Until You Become Fluent
Now that you have finished step five, and you can say every word correctly. Now repeat the whole chapter from the beginning to the end. Repeat for as many times as you need until you can say each sentence naturally and fluently.

Step 7: Record Your Voice
Now that you have finished step six, and you can say every word correctly and every sentence naturally and fluently. Now record your voice again. Record your voice repeating the same chapter. Save your file.

Find the first recording and listen to it. Then find the second recording and listen to it.

Did you speak better in the second recording than in the first recording?

> Yes? Take Step 8.
> No? Take Step 8.

Step 8: Move On To the Next Chapter
Listen to the audio of the next chapter and take steps 1 – 7.

After you've finished all chapters, go back to the first chapter and start over again until you speak this lesson like a native. After that, get that into your subconscious mind by practicing some more.

Look at the book the first few times, but after you're familiar with the text, put the book away. Just concentrate on the audio!

Chapter 3: Vowel Overview

There are five vowels in the English language. They are a, e, i, o, u. These vowels can combine with other vowels to form more vowel sounds.

To make our learning process easy, we'll use a simple way to learn the vowel sounds. Here is a list of the vowel sounds.

- E
- IH
- EH
- /æ/
- AH
- UH
- AW
- OH
- /ʊ/
- OO
- A
- I
- OW
- OY

There are two types of vowels – long vowel and short vowel.

The long vowels are
A, E, I, OY, OO, OH, OW

The short vowels are
IH, EH, /æ/, AH, UH, AW, /ʊ/

We'll get into each of them in details in the following chapters.

Chapter 4: The E sound.

Let's get familiar with the E sound. Try these words:

bee, deed, eat, feed, geese, he, jeans, keen, leap, meet, sneaker, tea, veal, wheel, yeast, zero.

E is a long vowel. Be sure to hold the sound long.

When the E sound is followed by a stop sound such as the /D/, the /T/, the /P/, the /M/ and so on, be sure to hold the E sound long before adding the stop sound.

Let's look at the word "deed." Here is how to pronounce it:
1. Say the vowel sound E long.
2. Add the ending /D/ sound. Now it becomes EED.
3. Add the beginning /D/ sound. Now the sound becomes DEED.

For the word "seem," do the same:
1. Say the vowel sound E long.
2. Add the ending /M/ sound.
3. Add the beginning /S/ sound. SEEM.

Same thing for the word "backseat." Say E long, then EAT, then SEAT, then "backseat."

To pronounce the E sound, smile. Place our tongue high and let it become tense. Pronounce the sound as we let the air out. E. E. E.

The E vowel sound can be formed from the following combinations. I have intentionally added a long list of words for us to practice. Here we go.

1. ee → agree, attendee, bee, beep, beetle, bleed, breed, career, cheek, cheer, cheese, cheetah, creek, creepy, deep, eighteen, exceed, esteem, feed, feel, fleet, free, freeze, foresee, freeway, Greece, green, greet, guarantee, heel, indeed, Jeep, keel, keen, keep, knee, levee, meet, need, needle, payee, peek, peel, peer, perigee, pioneer, queen, redeem, screen, seaweed, see, seed, sheep, sleepy, speech, speed, squeeze, sheer, steep, steer, succeed, sweep, sweet, teen, teenager, tree, trustee, tweet, weed, week, wheel

2. ea → backseat, beach, beam, bean, beast, beat, beaver, beneath, bleach, breathe, clean, clear, creak, cream, creature, defeat, disappear, dream, each, eagle, ear, east, easy, eat, fear, feast, gear, gleam, glean, hear, heat, heave, ideal, increase, leach, lead, leader, leaf, leave, least, meal, mean, near, neat, peace, peach, peak, peanut, pear, reach, read, real, reap, tea, teach, team, weave

3. ie and ei → achieve, believe, brief, brownie, ceiling, chief, cookie, either, ether, field, fierce, freebie, leisure, niece, piece, perceive, receipt, receive, shield, retrieve, seize

4. final e → be, he, me, she, we

5. final y → ability, actually, astronomy, automatically, baby, Billy, biology, chilly, city, copy, economy, family, frankly, funny, geography, grammatically, handy, Henry, huckleberry, January, Jenny, jewelry, kitty, lady, lucky, many, nanny, opportunity, puppy, silly, solemnly, solely, sunny, totally

6. final ey → alley, Bailey, barley, chimney, donkey, gooey, honey, joey, journey, key, money, monkey,

parsley, pulley, smiley, Smokey, turkey, valley, volley
7. final ique → antique, boutique, critique, oblique, technique, unique
8. e + consonant + e → Chinese, Japanese, Pete, Portuguese, Sudanese, these, Vietnamese

Now let's practice the E vowel sound in sentences.
1. Friend A, "A friend in need is a friend indeed."
2. Friend B, "Agreed! Give me your money."
3. Come with me. You'll be surprised what we'll see although your safety is not guaranteed.
4. Attendees are free to bring creepy crawlies, beetles, and bees. Feel free to watch them feast or become their feed.
5. Walk up to this peak of eighteen feet in high heels to see how you'll feel.
6. Feed a mouse cheese, and the mouse will be happy.
7. Feed a cheetah cheese, and the cheetah will make you bleed.
8. Give a monkey a peach, and the monkey will be crazy.
9. Give a monkey a speech, and the monkey will be sleepy.
10. My donkey loves barley.
11. My honey loves money.
12. Take a seat on the beach and feed the seals beans.
13. Take the heat to succeed and scream out our dreams
14. Beasts feast at ease.
15. Peace reaches east.
16. Free breeze greets our cheeks. Feel the heat. Keep on going until you succeed.
17. Say "Cheese!" Take a picture in the deep creek.
18. Both teams agree to meet at three thirty.
19. In this city, green tea is easy to see.
20. January is my favorite month to study astronomy.
21. Every month is my honey's favorite month to buy jewelry.
22. When Emily feels chilly, she goes back to her family.
23. When Henry meets opportunities, he heaves fiercely.

Chapter 5: The Slightly Different IH Sound

Let's feel the sound.

Acid, bit, dig, fill, fit, hill, Jill, kid, lip, pig, Rick, win

IH is a short vowel. Remember the vowel E sound that we have to keep the sound long? The IH sound is the opposite. It's short.

Let's look at the word "acid." Here is how to pronounce it:
1. Say the vowel sound IH short.
2. Then add the closing /D/ sound. Now it becomes IHD.
3. Then add the "c" which is the /S/ sound, so now its sound becomes CIHD."
4. Finally, add the beginning /æ/ sound. /æ/CIHD.

For the word "bid," do the same:
1. Say the vowel sound IH short.
2. Add the closing /D/ sound, so now it becomes IHD.
3. Add the beginning /B/ sound, so now its sound becomes BIHD."

To pronounce IH, relax our lips, slightly open them, and relax our tongue. Let the air out. IH, IH, IH. Remember how to say *it*? Say *it* without the T ending. IH, IH, IH.

This vowel can be formed by the following combinations. Again, I have listed a long list of words. Let's practice them:

1. i → acid, bid, big, bin, bring, brink, bit, chicken, chilly, chip, Cindy, disk, dictionary, did, different, dig, dim, dinner, dip, exit, fiction, finger, figure, fix, gift, hiccup, hidden, Hilary, hill, him, hint, hippo, his, hitch, immune, international, interesting, investment, itself, Jill, kick, kid, Kimberly, kin, kit, lid, lily, list, listen, lizard, mixture, music, outfit, picture, pig, pin, pit, rich, rip, risk, silk, silly, single, sip, swing, ticket, Tiffany, tilt, tip, unit, video, wing, which, wizard
2. ui → biscuit, build, circuit, guilt
3. y between consonants → cylinder, encryption, decryption, gym, gymnastics, gypsy, hymn, Lynch, Lynn, mystic, mystery, myth, mythology, rhythm, syllable, symbol

Now let's practice them in sentences.

1. Bring a big bin of acid. Drink none of it because it's toxic.
2. Put six bids on the acid but do not spit on the acid.
3. Chilly chips in the fifth bin. Silly gifts in the sixth bin.
4. Fix the circuit with this drill bit.
5. Eat an olive make sure to spit the pit.
6. A dictionary on a disk is handy. Digging fictions for vocabulary is history.
7. Hilary and Kimberly are taking different exits. Hilary is going to a hill. Kimberly is going to the Hills'.
8. Hidden hippos hiccup and kick. Glittering lizards hitch and lift.
9. Invest little, go to Chicago. Invest big, go international.
10. This outfit makes me look rich. Kiss risks to succeed.
11. Feed pigs biscuits, and pigs will like it. Let pigs listen to music, and pigs will fall asleep.
12. Rich witches sit by the fire pit.
13. Bill fills the mill he built with milk. Then he mills the milk and tilts the mill until mill spills.
14. I built my guilt in quivers when I decrypted the symbols encrypted by UFOs.
15. The circus is quickly filled with children.
16. Mitt quizzes the hymn in the gym.

Let's compare the two sounds. The IH sound is similar to the E sound, but its pronunciation is slightly different.

Try these two words:
seat
sit

Do they sound different or the same? How about these two:
feet
fit

And these two:
sheep
ship

These sets of word sound very similar, but they do sound slightly different. Let's first detect the differences and then pronounce the differences.

For the words seat, feet, and sheep, the "ea" and "ee" have the E sound, and the sound is long. E. E. E

To say it correctly, our lips should be tense, wide, and look like we're smiling. What do photographers say when they're taking pictures? "Say cheese." That's because the "ee" in "cheese" make us look like we're smiling, and the sound of "ee" is long.

For the words sit, fit, and ship, the IH sound is short. Our lips should be relaxed and narrow. Our tongue should also be relaxed. It should also be high and be touching our upper teeth.

IH is a short vowel. It's always closed by a consonant such as in sit, fit and ship, it's closed by /T/ and /P/.

Now let's give them a try.

bean, bin
beat, bit
dean, din
deed, did
deem, dim
deep, dip
ease, is
feast, fist
feel, fill
feet, fit
glean, glint
green, grin
he's, his
heal, hill
heat, hit
keen, kin
keep, kip
lead, lid
leak, lick
least, list
leave, live
mead, mid
meal, mill
mean, min
meet, Mitt
peak, pick
peel, pill
reach, rich
read, rid
sheep, ship

Now let's practice E and IH together.

1. Six ships ship six sheep when the sheep are asleep.

2. You're welcome to trim your feet to fit the shoes or to trim the shoes to fit your feet.

3. Mitt places the seat in front of the pit and sits with Mick.

4. Jim put the beans in the bin when the room was dim and deemed a joyful hymn.

5. Climb the hill in high heels to see how you'll feel.

6. Watching out for bees when you play Frisbee is tricky but easy.

7. Eat it or leave it.

8. Take a seat and sit down.

9. Fill the cup with hot water and feel the heat.

10. Which peak do you pick? The Reed Hill or the Rid Hill.

11. Fill the mill with milk then feed the eel a meal.

Chapter 6: The Easy EH Sound

Let's first get a feel of the EH sound:

bed, beckon, desk, egg, festival, get, hen, Jenny, Ken, lend, pet, vest, west

To pronounce EH, relax our lips, relax our tongue and raise it from mid to high position and let the air out. EH. EH. EH.

To pronounce the words, pronounce them backward.

Bed → EH, EHD, BEHD.
Bread → EH, EHD, REHD, BREHD.

EH is a short vowel. It's always closed by a consonant.

The EH sound can be formed from the following combinations:
1. e → beckon, bed, best, celebrate, decorate, dedicate, definition, den, detect, effect, egg, excel, excellent, February, fence, festival, gemstone, generate, get, guest, hen, Henry, Jeff, Jenny, jet, left, leg, let, levy, meditate, memory, men, mess, met, Neptune, nest, next, peck, peddle, pen, pencil, pepper, pet, quest, replicate, rest, restaurant, segment, semester, sense, September, settle, success, technique, technology, Ted, temperature, ten, tennis, test, text, vest, Wednesday, welcome, Wendy, west, yesterday, yet
2. ea → ahead, bear, bread, dread, feather, heavy, instead, meadow, measure, read (past tense), spread, treadmill, weather
3. These exceptions → again, against, any, many, said, says (when the word "say" is in the present tense third person such as "She says she wants to.)

Now let's practice them in sentences.

1. Step on Neptune questing for effect. There is no ground there so leave like a jet.

2. Celebrate a festival with eggs and pets if you want them to make a mess.

3. Henry and Jenny meditate to retain memory.

4. Two woodpeckers met. They ate and left.

5. I still have my best vest left. I'll wear it to my success.

6. What's heavier? They hit the ground together.

7. To help you speak like a native, repeat the sentences again and again and then again and again.

8. How many times do I expect to try until my success?

9. Practice again and again all the way to the end when you pronounce like Ken and then do it again.

10. General Fred said he sent Henry west to select the best vest for success.

11. The first step is to set a goal on what you want next.

12. Then settle and write down what you want to get.

13. Finally, send our energy like a jet, measure how far they spread, eat some bread, and push through to our success.

Chapter 7: The Stronger /æ/ Sound

Let's hear the sound.

Add, bat, cat, dad, fathom, hat, jacket, ladder, matter, nap, path, rather, saddle, tackle, vast

What sound does a goat make?

That's the sound. Our jaw drops down as we make the sound.

Let's try to pronounce /æ/:
Back → /æ/, /æ/CK, B/æ/CK.

To pronounce /æ/, open our lips, lower our tongue, open our mouth wide and drop our jaw as we let the air out. /æ/. /æ/. /æ/.

/æ/ is also a short vowel. It's always closed by a consonant.

The /æ/ sound can only be formed from the letter a:
  1. a → add, adequate, apple, back, cab, cafeteria, calendar, camp, candle, candy, cast, Cathy, dash, family, fantastic, fast, fathom, gadget, galaxy, gallon, gas, gather, had, half, hamster, hand, happen, has, hatch, have, jab, jam, Jasper, kangaroo, Kathrine, ladder, mad, man, map, mask, master, pack, pad, pan, pant, past, pat, plan, plateau, practice, prank, ram, ran, raspberry, rather, sack, sand, Saturday, tackle, tag, tan, tango, value, vast, wagon

Now let's practice them in sentences.

1. Add an adequate amount of gas and activate the plant. Let's watch this technology advance.

2. Technology is going to be a handy gadget.

3. Attention, gang. Bring some candles, candy, pans, and pants. We are going to camp.

4. Standing in front of a mirror, I looked like a lamb.

5. The good thing was I still had an apple on my hand.

6. I laughed and ran because I had a goal and a plan.

7. I've tried and failed like a product without a brand.

8. At last, I cried like an ant, thinking this was my last chance.

9. A man handed me a book, it was Think and Grow Rich.

10. "I have an answer," said the man, "that failure is the mother of success, and the darkest moment is right before dawn. Persist and success will be in our hand."

11. I kept my goal, gather info from the book, and hatched a new plan.

12. Following the plan, my dream had advanced.

13. My goal was achieved, so I thanked the man and danced.

Now let's compare the differences between the EH sound and the /æ/ sound.

- bet, bat
- dense, dance
- fen, fan
- fest, fast
- guess, gas
- head, had
- Jen, Jan
- kept, capt
- lend, land
- men, man
- peddle, paddle
- rend, rand
- settle, saddle
- text, tax
- vest, vast
- west, wax

If we want to learn how to swim, memorizing a truckload of instructions will not get us there. The only way to learn to swim is to get into the water and swim. Keep practicing.

- bread, brat
- beck, back
- bend, band
- dread, draft
- expensive, expansive
- leg, lag
- letter, latter
- medal, waddle
- mess, mass
- pen, pan
- send, sand
- spend span
- spread, sprat
- ten, tan

- tread, trad

Now let's practice EH and /æ/ in the same sentences.

1. A homeless man standing ahead begging for money was carrying a tent.

2. I gave him a $100 bill, and he said nothing or bent.

3. "This book says no matter what shape you're in, you can still figure out a way to get your life back," said the man.

4. I recognized the book at a glance.

5. "You seem to be a successful man. Is there anything you can do to get my life back?" continued the man.

6. He was about to give up his life I sensed, "To get your life back? I'm sorry, I can't."

7. "This is the last thing I wanted to know before I leave. I'm better off just come back another time then."

8. "Sir, I'm not finished yet. There's nothing I can do to get your life back, but I know one man who can."

9. "Look here," I said as I pointed with my hand.

10. "This is the man who can help you with everything you want. Ask this man!"

11. As the homeless man looked to the front, he saw standing in front of him a homeless man with jacket dirty, hair messy, and skin tanned.

12. "This is the only man in the whole world who can help you to get your life back." I pointed at his reflection on the glass door and said in the present tense.

13. "This man has lost his soul. How can he help me?" The man was thoughtful for a moment and said with his head bent.

14. "He lost his soul because he lost his purpose for life. Give him a purpose to live for and he'll give you everything you ask for. Failure is the mother of success, and the darkest moment is right before dawn. Persist and success will be in your hand."

15. The man mused for a while, looked at the man in the glass from head to toe and from toe to head. He then turned to me and said, "Yes, sir. I'll give this man a purpose to live for." He then walked away like a product with a brand.

16. I met this homeless man again.

17. "I've gotten myself a purpose and a job for $10,000 a month!" He said proudly, "I just wanted to find you and tell you that I've found a bigger purpose for life and I, too, will one day be a successful man!"

Chapter 8: The AH Sound

Let's hear it:

alarm, car, doctor, economy, father, got, hard, hot, job, knob, lot, mother, toddler, robot

To pronounce AH, relax our lips, relax our tongue and place it on the floor of our mouth. AH.

Let's try pronouncing it:
Swab → AH, AHB, WAHB, SWAHB.

The AH sound can be formed from the following combinations:
1. a → alarm, archeology, arm, barn, calm, car, cartoon, cauliflower, charcoal, charge, Chicago, dark, far, farcical, farmer, father, garage, garbage, garden, garlic, garment, garnish, ha, hard, hardcover, hark, harm, harmonica, harness, harvest, mark, Mars, palm, swab, swap, target, wad, wand, want, watch, watt
2. o → astonish, Bobby, bobcat, bobtail, body, bond, box, clock, cop, cod, coddle, comic, combination, comedy, comet, common, document, doll, goggle, got, hollow, honest, honor, hop, hotshot, job, Josh, knock, knot, lobster, locker, modern, mop, nonstop, not, option, opportunities, pollen, polish, pocket, possible, rock, rotten, robot, solid, solve, solvent, stop, stock, toddler, Tom, tonic, top, topic
3. e → encore, entree, envelope, sergeant
4. ow → acknowledge, knowledge

Now let's talk about the AH sound and the AH + R sound.
ah, arh
ha, har
la, lar
ma, mar
spa, spar

With R, the AH sound now has the /R/ sound at the end. Ah becomes AHR.

Let's practice more words with the AHR sound:
alarm, apart, arc, arch, architecture, arm, art, barley, car, card, cardinal, cargo, carpet, cartoon, chart, dark, darling, depart, guard, hard, jar, large, mark, park, part, party, sarcasm, sardine, spar, spark, star, start, startle, tar, target

Now let's practice the AH sound in sentences.

1. Archaeologists were alarmed when an archaic barn was excavated from a farm.
2. Stay calm in the barn. There is no harm.
3. Bring cauliflowers in the car along with our harmonica.
4. Learn from someone next to you, not from someone far.
5. If your father is successful, model your father.
6. Plant seeds in your garden and harvest like a farmer.
7. Harness your power and garnish your car.
8. Astonished, boggled, and startled, Bobby was shocked as he watched the clock.
9. Time has passed for him to play with Josh.
10. Bobby laughed, "Common combinations for comics and comedies are stories, characters, and garbage."
11. Josh is one hotshot. He's honest, and he likes his job.
12. Josh likes to jog. He likes to hop as he jogs.
13. Josh jogs nonstop. He jogs in the dark and hops for nocturnal bugs.
14. Josh has a modern mop. A mop that he uses to polish rocks.
15. He has an option to fold the mop and put it in his pocket like a robot.
16. Tom is a volunteer in his shop. He has many opportunities to get to the top.

Chapter 9: The Similar UH Sound

Try the following pairs of words to see if they sound the same or different.

cot, cut
fond, fund

If we think these pairs are pronounced the same, congratulations! We are with the majority of ESL learners.

The fact is, they are pronounced different! One is AH. The other is UH.

Let's get familiar with the UH sound:

Ana, banana, but, cut, cousin, done, enough, fun, gut, hut, just, love, honey, monkey, rough, tough, young

To pronounce UH, relax our lips, relax our tongue and place it in the middle position, slightly open our mouth as we let the air out. UH. UH. UH.

For the AH sound, our mouth is wide open. For the UH sound, our mouth is slightly open. Let's compare the sounds.

AH, UH
AH, UH
AH, UH

Let's try it.
Cut → UH, UHT, CUHT.
Enough → UH, UHF, NUHF, ENUHF.

The UH sound can be formed from the following combinations:

1. a → Alabama, America, Ana, Asia, banana, Canada, China, Cuba, drama, fuchsia, Georgia, hyena, Jessica, Katrina, Lisa, mama, sonata, panda, umbrella, utopia, was, zebra
2. o → above, another, brother, color, cover, come, complete, computer, does, done, from, honey, love, Monday, money, monkey, mother, of, other, oven, shove, sophisticated, son, ton, tongue
3. u → buddy, buck, buckle, buffalo, bug, bus, buzz, cup, cut, drunk, fun, hub, huddle, hung, jungle, lump, mud, mug, numb, pump, rum, sum, yummy
4. ou → country, cousin, enough, rough, tough, young

Now let's practice UH in sentences.

1. Alabama, Alaska, Arizona and Georgia are four states in America.
2. Ana lives in America. She has a good friend named Barbara.
3. Ana came from China. Barbara came from Cuba.
4. Ana likes fuchsia. Barbara likes magenta.
5. Jessica and Virginia dream to live in Utopia.
6. Katrina and Alisa like to drive a Sonata.
7. Throw a banana at a zebra. The zebra will buzz.
8. Throw a banana at a monkey. The monkey will go bananas.
9. Throw a banana at a panda. The panda will throw you back the banana.
10. Above the book cover is another color.
11. Your brother completed building the computer.
12. It is done and your brother is gone.
13. My honey loves money.
14. The oven will come on Monday.
15. If your mother is successful, learn from your mother.
16. Buckle up, buddy! We need to watch out for bucks, bugs, and buffaloes.
17. If you hear a buzz on the bus, get ready for a bump.
18. Huddle around and watch a drama for fun.
19. Running into the jungle with no shoes is fun, only if you'll bring your cousin and your son.

Now let's compare the difference between AH and UH.
a bar, above
alarm, a lump
Arthur, other
barn, bun
body, buddy
boggle, buckle
box, bucks
bother, brother
bars, bus
carver, cover
calm, come
collar, color
cop, cup
cot, cut
darts, does
darn, done
hop, hub
fond, fund
mark, mug
mod, mud
palm, pump
shop, shove
stop, stuff

Chapter 10: The AW Sound

Let's hear it.

awesome, author, August, bought, caught, fought, law, sought, wrought

To pronounce AW, slightly tense our lips, slightly tense our tongue and place it down near the floor of our mouth, slightly round our lips to an oval shape as we let the air out. AW. AW. AW.

Let's try it:
caught → AW, AWT, CAWT.
Frog → AW, AWG, RAWG, FRAWG.

The AW sound can be formed from the following combinations:
1. al → all, alter, altogether, always, ball, call, chalk, fall, gall, hall, install, mall, stalk, stall, tall, thrall, walk, wall
2. au → applaud, auction, audio, audit, Audrey, August, author, authorize, automatic, autograph, authentic, Aurora, authority, autumn, cause, faucet, haul, maul, Paul, pause, sauce
3. aught → aught, caught, daughter, naught
4. o → blog, boss, clog, dog, frog, hog, log, long, loss, lost, off, office, often, on
5. ought → bought, fought, ought, sought, thought, wrought
6. aw → awesome, brawn, claw, crawl, dawn, draw, fawn, flawless, jaw, jigsaw, hawk, law, lawn, lawyer, paw, prawn, raw, saw, slaw, straw, thaw

Now let's practice AW sentences

1. Ms. Thrall called Ms. Hall in the mall for more chalks.

2. Rinse your mouth with saltwater.

3. My learning will continue like a waterfall. It will never halt.

4. To play racquetball, always hit the ball to the wall and that's all.

5. Audrey automatically authorized the author of **Autumn Aurora** her authentic autograph in her automobile without auditions from the authority.

6. Paul applauds for the audio because the actress is his daughter.

7. Ross lost the password of the blog of his boss.

8. The dog, the frog, and the hog clogged the drain with a log.

9. Awesome! He quickly draws a picture of a hawk, a macaw, and a prawn on his lawn at dawn.

Chapter 11: The OH Sound

Let's hear the sound:
boat, coat, close, goat, low, gold, bowl, though, pole, oh, hold, wrote, own, window

To pronounce OH, tense our lips, slightly tense our tongue and move it from the middle position to the high position as we round our lips to let the air out. OH. OH. OH.

Let's try it:
Woke → OH, OHK, WOHK.
Encroach → OH, OHCH, ROHCH, CROHCH, ENCROHCH.

The OH sound is commonly formed from the following combinations:
1. o → ago, also, code, cold, close, dole, fold, go, gold, hello, hold, home, hope, modem, mold, mole, node, note, oh, old, open, over, phone, pole, roll, so, sold, soldier, told, toll, troll, whole, zone
2. oa → afloat, approach, boat, cloak, coach, coal, coast, coat, cockroach, croak, encroach, float, foam, goal, goat, load, loaf, moan, oak, oath, raincoat, reproach, roach, road, soak, soap, roam, throat, toad, toast
3. ough → although, borough, dough, doughnut, furlough, thorough, though, trough
4. ow → arrow, barrow, below, blow, bow, bowl, burrow, crow, elbow, fellow, flow, glow, grow, hollow, know, low, bone marrow, narrow, mow, own, pillow, rainbow, row, shallow, show, shown, slow, snow, sparrow, stow, throw, tow, window, yellow

Let's practice OH in sentences

1. This home was sold a whole year ago.

2. The note and the only gold were also sold.

3. People on the go picked up the phone to say hello.

4. To be so cold, wear no clothes, fold your arms, and roll your body in the snow.

5. To be successful, be bold. Focus on your goal and pay the toll.

6. With a goal, I have an approach.

7. Without a goal, I'm a rudderless boat afloat.

8. So, set a goal, take an oath, bring a raincoat, and get on the road.

9. Thank you, coach! You're welcome, my fellow.

10. Although there's a hole in a doughnut, you eat the doughnut, not the hole.

11. The moon is hollow, and its shell is shallow?

12. Hold your arrow to the burrow because UFOs come from below.

13. Lights glow often at your telescope.

14. Rice grows slowly toward yellow.

15. Sparrows will eat your rice, crows will stare at UFOs.

16. Bring a pillow, sit in a shadow by the window, lower your elbows, and enjoy a show.

Let's compare the sounds of AW and OH:

- all, old
- alter, older
- bald, bold
- bought, boat
- call, coal
- chalk, choke
- claws, close
- cloth, clothes
- craw, crow
- draw, drove
- fall, fold
- fought, fold
- gall, go
- hall, hole
- jaw, Joe
- law, low
- lawn, loan
- loss, Low's
- mall, mole
- Paul, poll
- paw, pole
- raw, row
- saw, sow
- slaw, slow
- sought, sold
- stall, stole
- tall, told
- thaw, though
- thought, though
- thrall, throw
- walk, woke

The more you practice, the better you get. Here are more.

- applause, approach

- awe, oh
- called, cold
- cause, coach
- crawl, croak
- flawless, float-less
- pall, poll
- Shaw, show
- tossed, toast
- wall, wolf

Chapter 12: The Pay-Attention /ʊ/ Sound

Let's hear the sound:

book, bush, cook, could, foot, full, good, hood, look, pull, should, wood

To pronounce /ʊ/, round our lips, relax our tongue and raise the back of it. /ʊ/. /ʊ/. /ʊ/.

Try to pronounce it:
Cook → /ʊ/, /ʊ/K, K/ʊ/K.
Understood → /ʊ/, /ʊ/D, T/ʊ/D, ST/ʊ/D, DERST/ʊ/D, UNDERST/ʊ/D.

/ʊ/ is a short vowel. It's always closed by a consonant.

The /ʊ/ sound can be formed from the following combinations:
1. oo → adulthood, afoot, audiobook, boogie, book, childhood, cook, cookbook, cookie, crook, foot, football, good, goody, hood, hook, look, rook, shook, snook, stood, stook, strook, took, understood, wood
2. ould → could, should, would
3. u → bull, bulletin, bush, full, fuller, pull, pullet, pulley, pullover, push, put

Now let's practice /ʊ/ in sentences.

1. Listen to an audiobook while we cook!

2. Find the ingredients of the cookies in a cookbook.

3. During their childhood life, read to your children good books.

4. Walk our journey on foot.

5. Football is meant to be played by foot.

6. Push the crooked hook to make it look good.

7. Look! There are goodies under the hood.

8. The rook shook the book and stood on a snook.

9. She understood the structure of woods.

10. He said he would if he could.

11. Should this bulletin be put next to the wood?

12. Mr. Fuller's bull, Fully, pushed the bush.

Let's compare the sounds of /ʊ/ and OH:

- book, boat
- cook, coke
- crook, croak
- foot, fold
- good, gold
- hood, hold
- hook, hope
- look, load
- rook, roll
- stood, stowed
- stook, stoke
- could, cold
- should, showed
- **bull, bowl**
- bush, boast
- **full, fold**
- **pull, poll**
- **pullet, pole it**
- **pulley, Polly**
- push, post
- put, poled

Now practice the following pairs again. Practice them carefully. They are different!

- **Bull, bowl,**
- **full, fold**
- **pull, pole**
- **pullet, pole it**
- **pulley, Polly**

Chapter 13: The Common OO Sound

Try the following pairs of words to see if they sound the same or different.

foot, food
look, Luke

If we think these pairs are pronounced the same, congratulations! We are with the majority of ESL learners.

The good news is, they are pronounced different! One is /ʊ/. The other is OO.

Let's get familiar with the OO sound:

bloom, blue, chew, clue, choose, do, duty, food, goose, mood, move, moon, ruler, super, who, zoo

Let's try to pronounce it:
Andrew → OO, ROO, DROO, ANDROO.
Food → OO, OOD, FOOD.

To pronounce OO, round our lips. Our lips are rounded like a circle. Relax our tongue and raise the back of it as we let the air out. OO. OO. OO.

What sound does an owl make? That's the sound. OO is a long vowel. Make sure to hold the sound long.

The OO sound is commonly formed from the following combinations:
1. ew → Andrew, blew, brew, cashew, chew, crew, dew, flew, grew, jewelry, jewels, screw, stew, threw
2. o → approve, do, doable, loose, lose (I intentionally put these two together. Listen for the difference and then speak the difference.), move, movable, movie,

prove, redo, remove, removable, reprove, shoe, to, two, undo, who, whose

3. oo → afternoon, baboon, balloon, bamboo, bloom, boo, boot, booth, broom, carpool, choose, cocoon, cooed, cool, food, droop, gloomy, goof, Google, goose, groove, hoof, hoot, kangaroo, lagoon, loop, loose, lose, (Did you hear the difference earlier? The difference is the ending S and Z sounds. We'll get to them in details in a later chapter.), loot, maroon, mood, moon, moot, moose, noodle, noon, ooze, pool, proof, roof, room, school, scoop, scoot, shampoo, smooth, snooze, soon, spoon, sooth, spook, too, tool, tooth, zoo

4. u → Bruce, bruise, conclude, crude, cruise, dual, dune, duty, fluid, flute, fruit, include, juice, June, lube, plume, prudence, prudential, prune, recruit, revolution, rule, ruler, spruce, student, suit, super, through, tube, tune

5. ue → avenue, blue, clue, cruel, due, duel, flue, glue, pursue, statue, Sue, Tuesday

6. Words with the U sound → amuse, argue, barbecue, beautiful, continue, cube, cue, cute, excuse, few, fuel, fuse, hue, huge, human, humidity, humor, issue, knew, menu, muse, music, mute, new, Newton, nuclear, pew, preview, pure, queue, renew, rescue, review, skew, tissue, U-turn, UFO, unit, unite, unicorn, unicycle, uniform, unique, universe, use, usually, Utah, utensil, venue, view

Now let's practice OO in sentences.

1. Andrew blew away the cashew he chewed.
2. The brew crew drew dew as they flew.
3. New jewels were approved as the jewelry store grew.
4. Newton knew why apples drooped.
5. His universal rule: loose objects moved downward as you threw.
6. Approved! Utah's carpool plan is cool! It's doable, movable, and usable, too.
7. If you lose your shoes, fetch them with a bamboo.
8. What color do you choose this afternoon, blue or maroon?
9. Where do you plan to go tomorrow, a hot air balloon, a lagoon, or the moon?
10. Today, tomorrow, tonight, love together, humanity unites.
11. Sue and Drue choose the gloomy booth to barbecue the food.
12. So true! They ate noodles in the pool.
13. Set the goose loose to let it fly to the roof of the igloo.
14. This zoo is a valuable tool for schools.
15. The peekaboo moon spooked the moose, too.
16. Stay tuned on Channel 2 if you want to hear the true sound of this muted flute.
17. Bruce's bruise suits his effort on what he's been through.
18. June is the time to take a cruise.
19. If you want to pass through, drink some juice. That's the rule.

Now let's compare /ʊ/ and OO.

/ʊ/ OO
/ʊ/ OO

book, boot
bush, booth
cook, cool
could, cooled
foot, food
full, fool
goods, goose
hood, hoot
look, Luke
pull, pool
pullet, prove it
pushed, boost
rook, rule
shook, shoe
should, shoot
snooks, snooze
stood, stewed
strook, strew
sugar, shooter
took, tool

Now do the following pairs again. Practice them carefully. They are different!

foot, food
full, fool
hood, hoot
look, Luke
pull, pool
should, shoot
stood, stewed

Chapter 14: The Easy A Sound

Let's hear the sound:

able, baby, cake, day, eighteen, faith, gave, hay, innate, jade, Kate, lemonade, make, okay, prepaid, quake, statement, take, way

To pronounce the A sound, relax our lips, tense our tongue, and move our tongue up. A. A. A.

Let's try it:
Cable → A, ABL, KABL.
Brain → A, AN, RAN, BRAN.

The A sound can be formed from the following combinations:
1. a → able, abrasive, administrator, aliens, alligator, angel, April, baby, cable, canine, capable, danger, delegation, David, fable, gable, hallucination, maple, nation, naval, recommendation, staple, table, vapor
2. a + consonant + e → abdicate, accumulate, ace, ache, adjacent, age, amaze, bakery, belated, blade, cadence, cape, change, chase, date, delegate, engage, exaggerate, exhale, fade, fate, gate, grade, handshake, haze, hazelnut, inhale, James, Jane, Kate, lake, make, mandate, methane, navy, pavement, quake, rate, relate, save, skate, take, wake
3. ai → acclaim, acquaintance, afraid, aid, aim, available, await, bail, brain, Cain, chain, claim, contain, daily, detail, domain, email, entertain, explain, faith, gain, hail, Jaiden, Kaiden, mailbox, maintain, mermaid, nail, obtain, pain, plain, praise, quail, raincoat, raise, retain, sail, snail, sprain, straight, tail, tailor, trail, train, trait, vain, wait, waive,
4. ay → array, away, Ayers, bay, cay, day, delay, Fayetteville, Gayle, Hayden, Jay, Kay, lay, May, payday, ray, say, way
5. ea → break, great, steak, unbreakable,

6. ei → eight, beige, freight, neighbor, reign, rein, sleigh, unveil, veil, vein, weight
7. ey → fey, Grey, hey, prey, survey, they

Let's practice A in sentences.

1. Yesterday has gone away.

2. Tomorrow is not yet awake.

3. Face today with bravery, use every second you've saved, and build your English pronunciation today!

4. To be successful, I must face pain. I've failed so much that pain can no longer hurt my brain.

5. I get up straight away, even if my ankle was sprained.

6. I keep walking toward my target, despite the hail and the rain.

7. Dedicate and be brave. Your plan can change; your goal must remain.

8. With faith, even water can cut through rocks. Hey! Keep working, and your effort will be repaid.

9. Is it an alien or my hallucination? April and Angel, what are your recommendations?

10. David, the fable illustrator, is capable of illustrating maples on tables.

11. Amazing! Alligators are chasing prey in the naval base.

12. Delegate when your work accumulates. Save a day and go straight to the gate of aid.

13. Conduct a survey, aim at a place, engage and participate, make mistakes, exchange handshakes, go straight, and success awaits.

14. James, Jane, and Kate swam in the lake.

15. Exaggerate! Decorating her skates with chains.

16. Titan's air contains methane. The moon of Saturn is a domain waiting to be claimed.

17. Take the train to Spain to find James Cain. If he's not there, harvest a sugar cane.

18. Jaiden, Hayden, and Kaiden singing in cadence for entertainment.

19. Jay and Kay cooperate in a relay race to aim for first place.

20. Great! Let's take an eight-minute break, and perhaps we can lose some weight.

Chapter 15: The I Sound

First, let's hear the sound:

bye, cycle, dime, eye, fly, guy, hi, ice, jive, kite, life, mind, nice, rice, sight, time, vine

To pronounce I, say AH and then E together. Our mouth should be opened wide on AH and then slowly closing for E. Our tongue should be flat on the bottom and then raise to high position. I. I. I.

Let's try it:
Bike → I, IK, BIK.
Frighten → TEN, RITEN, FRITEN.

The I sound can be formed from the following combinations:
1. i → bike, biker, bicycle, biology, bite, citation, cite, dial, dice, dike dime, dine, diner, dive, diver, file, fine, five, giant, hi, hide, hike, hive, ice, iceberg, jive, kind, kite, knife, lice, life, light, like, lime, line, lite, live, mice, Michael, microphone, mile, mind, mine, miner, Niagara, nice, Nike, Nile, pike, pile, pine, pioneer, pipe, price, pride, primary, prime, quite, rice, ride, rifle, rile, Riley, ripe, ripen, rise, side, silent, smile, site, survive, swipe, size, tide, tie, tiger, tile, time, tiny, title, via, viable, vice, vine, vital, wide, while, white, wife, WIFI, wipe, wiper, viper, write, wise, yikes
2. ie → apple-pie, applies, bow-tie, butterflies, cries, cried, dragonflies, dries, flies, fries, fried, lie, magnifies, magnified, magpie, pie, replies, replied, skies, spied, spies, tie, tried, tries, untied
3. igh →bright, delight, fight, fighter, flight, fright, frighten, height, high, knight, light, lighthouse, might, mighty, moonlight, night, plight, right, sight, slight, sunlight, thigh, tight, tonight, twilight
4. y → apply, butterfly, buy, by, bye, comply, cry, cycle, dragonfly, dry, dye, eye, fly, fry, guy, hype, July, Kyle,

Lyle, magnify, my, ply, plywood, Popeye, pry, recycle, reply, Ryan, rye, shy, sky, spy, style, type, typhoon, xylophone, why

Now look at these words:
Tide, Tight
Side, Cite
Hide, Height

Do they sound the same to you? If you heard they sounded the same, congratulations! You're with the majority of ESL learners.

They are slightly different. Listen to how long the I sound is. Let's try them again.
Tide, Tight
Side, Cite
Hide, Height

In tide, side, and hide, the ones with longer vowel lengths and D endings, the length of the I sound is slightly longer. Listen to them again.
Tide, Tight
Side, Cite
Hide, Height

In tide, side, and hide, the ones with the D endings, the length of the I sound is longer. The length of the I sound is longer because these three words end with the /D/ sound. /D/ is a voiced consonant. We'll learn consonants in details in the later chapters of this book, but now, let's take a brief look at the voiced consonants.

The voiced consonants are:
/B/, /D/, /G/, /J/, /L/, /M/, /N/, /NG/, /R/, /TH/, /V/, /W/, /Y/, /Z/, /ZH/

When a word ends with one of these voiced consonants, we need to hold the vowel sound right before these consonants longer.

Did I say hold the vowel sound right before these consonants longer? Yes, I did. When a word ends with one of these voiced consonants, we need to hold the vowel sound longer right before these consonants.

Now let's try these three pairs one more time.
Tide, Tight
Side, Cite
Hide, Height

Here are more pairs of similar words for us to try. What do we do? Hold the vowel length before the voiced consonants longer!
Five, Fife
Live, Life
Bride, Bright
Size, Sights
Ride, Write
Knives, Knife
Eyes, Ice (The S in eyes is pronounced as /Z/, and /Z/ is a voiced consonant, therefore we hold the I sound longer.)

Again, we'll learn consonants and vowel lengths in details in the later chapters, but for now let's practice the I sound in sentences.

1. The biker on the bicycle is riding on the bike.
2. Cite your citations like taking your vacations for the biology class that you like.
3. Dial 9 then roll a dice to decide what side of the dike to dike.
4. Dine at Diner to have a bite and hire a driver with dimes.
5. Dive into the water when in a single file line then all divers will be fine.
6. Five giant bee hives are hiding behind the pine. All hikers are required to bring some ice.
7. An iceberg stopped the Titanic when some riders were dancing Jive.
8. This kind of kite looks like a knife.
9. Walk five miles if you don't mind to meet the miners in the mine.
10. Which one do you have in mind, Niagara Falls or the Nile River?
11. Pine cones pile up at Pioneer Market on Pike.
12. Take pride! The prime pipe is priced quite right.
13. Her rice has silently risen and ripen. What a sight!
14. Rice rises on site. Harvest from the right side on time. Imbibe to survive.
15. Swipe a tiger you'd better hide. Tigers are sized to fight worldwide.
16. It's viable to get a title via Tile Time. Just wear a white tie with a grapevine from a pine.
17. Wipe a viper with a wiper is wise only if you're truly prepared to die.
18. "Honey, if you want to get something tonight," said the wife, "it's vital we have WIFI all the time."
19. Butterflies, dragonflies, fruit flies, and magpies, fighting to enjoy the apple pie.
20. Magnify! Do you see the spy wearing a bow tie, lying supine, crossing the sky?
21. At midnight, under the moonlight, nine bright lights

light up the sky.
22. Kyle and Lyle, Popeye and Ryan, applied to dive a mile in July.
23. Right! The tide has reached its height by the lighthouse at twilight.
24. "An eye for an eye makes the world blind."
25. I say let's forgive and survive.

Chapter 16: The OW Sound

Let's get familiar with the OW sound:

around, bound, cloud, clown, found, house, how, sound, town, wow

To pronounce OW, say AH in a regular voice and OH in a lower voice. Our mouth should be opened wide on AH and then slowly closing and rounded on OH. OW. OW.

Let's try it:
Crouch → OW, OWCH, ROWCH, CROWCH.
Allow → OW, LOW, ALOW.

The OW sound can be formed from the following combinations:
1. ou → about, account, aloud, amount, announce, around, arouse, blouse, bounce, bound, boundary, cloud, couch, counselor, count, counter, countless, county, crouch, doubt, drought, en-route, flour, flounder, found, ground, grout, hound, hour, house, joust, loud, lounge, louse, lout, mound, mount, mountain, mouse, mouth, noun, ouch, ounce, our, oust, out, outcome, outdoors, outfit, output, pouch, pound, pout, proud, pronounce, round, rouse, route, scout, shout, snout, sound, soundless, soundtrack, south, spouse, spout, stout, stoutly, stoutness, surround, thousand, trout, tousle, vouch, voucher
2. ow → allow, allowance, anyhow, bow, Bowry, brow, brown, brownie, browse, browser, cauliflower, chow, chowder, clown, cow, cowboy, cowfish, crown, crowd, down, downhill, download, downstairs, downtown, dowry, drowsy, empower, endow, eyebrow, flower, fowl, frown, glower, gown, growl, how, howdy, however, howl, manpower, Mayflower, meow, now, owl, pow, power, Powell, powder, prowl, scowl, shower, towel, tower, town, trowel, vowel, vow, wow

Now let's practice the OW sound in sentences.

1. What's the amount in the account? Read aloud to announce to people around.
2. Arouse! Get up from the couch and bound for town.
3. Wow! The cloud is bouncing around.
4. How many people are heading to town? Can you count?
5. Of course, I can count! The cloud is bouncing around.
6. He mounted his horse to climb up the mountain.
7. After the drought, the mouse found a nesting ground.
8. If you have doubt, howl. You're a tiger if you're aroused from your couch.
9. Look out! There is a mouse!
10. Be proud! You're the man of the house!
11. Is it a noun or a pronoun? Who cares? Just pronounce the sound.
12. In this soundless mountain, there are thousands of trees around.
13. A scowled owl prowls the meadow.
14. Allowances will be allowed to spouse of the aroused.
15. Let's browse Mr. Brown's brownie shop with the crowd.
16. Don't frown. If empowered, even a cowboy can take the crown.
17. To download on this browser, go downhills to downtown.
18. Like the Mayflower, be the first and you're in power.
19. If you have power, you can shower in this tower.

Chapter 17: The OY Sound

Let's try the OY sound:

avoid, boy, choice, Doyle, enjoy, foil, hoist, joy, loyal, moisture, noise

To pronounce OY, Say AW and E together. That's AW EEE. Our mouth should be slightly rounded on AW and then slowly open wide for E. Our tongue should be relaxed in the middle position and then raise to the high position. OY. OY. OY.

Let's get it:
Detroit → OY, OYT, ROYT, TROYT, DETROYT.
Enjoy → OY, JOY, ENJOY.

The OY sound can be formed from the following combinations:
1. oi → Android, appoint, appointment, avoid, ballpoint, boil, boiler, broil, choice, coil, coin, Detroit, doily, enjoin, exploit, foil, groin, hoick, hoist, invoice, join, joint, loin, moil, moist, moisture, noise, noisy, oil, oink, point, poise, poison, recoil, rejoice, sirloin, soil, spoil, toil, voice, void
2. oy → alloy, annoy, boy, boyfriend, boyhood, convoy, cowboy, decoy, deploy, destroy, destroyer, employ, employee, employer, enjoy, Hoyle, joy, joyful, loyal, loyalty, oyster, ploy, royal, savoy, soy, soybean, toy, Troy, voyage, Voyager, zoysia

Now let's practice OY in sentences.
1. Appoint an android to avoid the asteroid.
2. Here is a pen with a ballpoint. Boil or broil, write down your choice.
3. The boiler is destroyed. Make an appointment, wrap it up with foil, and give it a hoist.
4. Rejoice when your plan is foiled. Exploit another opportunity and recoil.
5. Test erosion with a groin. Test your strength with a hoick.
6. Enjoy your broiled bok choy in Detroit! Here is your invoice.
7. Moil your point, toil your voice, brace for noise, and success is poised.
8. Oil the joint, fill the void, and cheer your joy.
9. Oink, oink. The pig house is moist. Bring some soil, and pigs will enjoy.
10. Recoil! Under the zoysia, a snake is coiled. It's employed. Make no noise.
11. Send a convoy with your envoy when you're poised to deploy.
12. Hoyle, the cowboy, who's loyal to Monroy, is in the convoy.
13. With some soy milk as a decoy, Hoyle the cowboy, enjoins a ploy.
14. Soybean and soy milk contain soy. Take some cabbage as savoy. Enjoy!
15. Boy! Joyce Roy, owner of a Roll-Royce, who sells toys, coins, and alloy, is voyaging to Troy.

Chapter 18: The /ER/ Sound

Let's hear the /ER/ sound:
bird, dirt, earth, girl, her, lurk, mercy, nerd, occur, perch, sir, turf, venture

The /ER/ sound is the sound of the vowels, a, e, i, o, u follow by the letter R.

How do we pronounce the word OR?
> It is O + R
> We pronounce it /O/ /R/
> When we say it quickly, its sound becomes /OR/, /OR/.
> Now faster, /OR/, /OR/

That's how we get the /ER/ sound. Vowel + the /R/ sound.

How do we pronounce the word YOUR?
> It is YOU + R
> We pronounce it /YOO/ /R/
> When we say it quickly, its sound becomes /YOOR/, /YOOR/.
> Now faster, /YOOR/, /YOOR/

The /ER/ sound can be formed from all five vowels, a, e, i, o, u, and their combinations plus /R/:

1. ar → binocular, blizzard, caterpillar, cellar, cellular, circular, collar, cougar, grammar, irregular, lizard, particular, polar, regular, sugar
2. er → archer, blender, carpenter, character, consider, dreamer, either, father, gather, her, insurer, joiner, keeper, lender, mercy, mother, reader, winner
3. ear → early, earn, earnest, earth, heard, learn, pearl, rehearse, research, search
4. ir → affirm, birth, circle, confirm, firm, first, girl, sir, shirt, skirt, smirk, stir, swirl, thirst, thirteen, Virginia,

virtual, virtues, whirl

5. or → actor, anchor, author, bachelor, chancellor, creator, doctor, editor, educator, equator, factor, gator, inventor, monitor, operator, simulator, visor, word

6. ur → absurd, burner, curtain, curve, exurbs, femur, fur, furnace, furniture, further, hurdle, nocturne, occur, turf

7. ure → adventure, culture, endure, ensure, exposure, feature, fixture, gesture, injure, insure, leisure, nature, obscure, posture, secure, venture

Chapter 19: The Dropped Vowel Sounds

Let's hear the sounds:
chocolate, family, final, interesting, restaurant, separate

In natural speaking, some vowels are dropped.

Let's take a look at a dropped vowel in the word "interesting."

The correct full pronunciation is "in-te-resting." However, in natural speaking, its pronunciation becomes "intresting." Both pronunciations are correct. When we say "interesting" at a natural speed, we say "intresting." When we say "interesting" at a slow speed, say "in-te-resting."

Dropping one or more vowels in words makes the words sound very natural.

So instead of saying "cho-co-late," say "choclit."
Instead of saying "fa-mi-ly," say "famly."

Let's practice them.
fi-nal → finl
in-te-resting → intresting
res-tau-rant → restrant
se-pa-rate → seprit

Again, in natural speaking, we completely drop the sound of some vowels. The good news is, there are very few of these words. When we hear someone says in-te-resting slowly, it's correct, too!

Chapter 20: The Reduced Vowel Sounds

We have just learned the dropped vowel sounds where we completely drop the sounds of some vowels.

Now let's learn the reduced vowel sounds. Let's hear the sounds:
Adjust, advance, along, alive, amaze, another

Have we noticed that we say
- əlong instead of a long?

Have we noticed that we say
- ənother instead of an other?

In reduced vowel sounds, we keep all the vowel sounds but reduce some vowel sounds.

To correctly pronounce the reduced vowel sounds, we do three things:
1. Lower the sound pitch.
2. Shorten the vowel length.
3. Lower the sound volume.

Let's hear them again. Look at the underlined letters.
Adjust, advance, along, alive, amaze, another

We reduce some vowel sounds to make some other vowel sounds stand out. Here are more.

accountant, accomplish, accumulate, Balloon, beautiful

Let's take balloon as an example. We say Balloon but not Ball Loon.

Let's try more.

Balloon, beautiful, camera, constant, construction, continue, electricity, gingerly, human, investigate, kilometer, personal, pedestrian, personify, photographer, residential, until, university

Again, to correctly pronounce the reduced vowel sounds, we do three things:
  1. Lower the sound pitch.
  2. Shorten the vowel length.
  3. Lower the sound volume.

Let's try them again.
Balloon, beautiful, camera, constant, construction, continue, electricity, gingerly, human, investigate, kilometer, personal, pedestrian, personify, photographer, residential, until, university

Again, we reduce some vowel sounds to make some other vowel sounds stand out.

Chapter 21: The Regular Vowel Sounds

The regular vowel sounds are the sounds we pronounce regularly.

So far we have learned
- the dropped vowel sounds
- the reduced vowel sounds
- the regular vowel sounds

Let's learn the last one – the stressed vowel sounds.

Chapter 22: The Stressed Vowel Sounds

We've learned the reduced vowel sounds. Now let's learn the opposite – the stressed vowel sounds.

Let's look at the following word.

Congratul**a**tions

Have we noticed that the highlighted vowel /A/ is stressed?

We say Congratul**a**tions but not C**o**ngrat**u**lati**o**ns?

We say s**e**ntence, not sent**e**nce.
We say Am**e**rica, not **A**meric**a**.

This is word stress. We stress the sound on some vowels and reduce the sound on some other vowels.

Let's try them again.
Congratul**a**tions
S**e**ntence
Am**e**rica

Stressed vowels are pronounced:
1. Higher in pitch
2. Longer in vowel length
3. May even be louder

Let's try them again.
Congratul**a**tions
S**e**ntence
Am**e**rica

Again, they're pronounced with a higher pitch, longer vowel length, and sometimes with a louder voice. Let's try them again.
Congratul**a**tions
S**e**ntence

America

Let's take a look at the following word.
America

There are four syllables in the word America – A, Me, Ri, Ca.
A – Reduced vowel sound, short vowel length
Me – Stressed vowel sound, long vowel length
Ri – Reduced vowel sound, short vowel length
Ca – Regular vowel sound, regular vowel length

Have we noticed that stressed vowels are the opposite of reduced vowels? Let's try it again.
America
America
America

How do I know which syllable to stress on? The good news is, there are many rules to follow although the rules don't always work. However, here is a rule that always work – learn the words.

Chapter 23: Intonation

Let's look at these four sentences.

1. They are coming.
2. **They** are coming.
3. They **are** coming.
4. They are **coming**.

These four sentences are identical, however, when we stress on different words, we get different meanings from the same sentence.

Look at the underlined words in the sentences. These are the stressed words.

1. They are coming. They are coming.
Nothing is stressed. It's just a normal sentence.

2. **They** are coming. **They** are coming.
It tells our listeners who are coming – they.

3. They **are** coming. They **are** coming.
It's about whether or not they are coming. Stress on the word *are* to tell our listeners that they are coming.

4. They are **coming**. They are **coming**.
It's about what they're doing. In this case, they are coming. Coming is their action. Coming is what they're doing.

This is intonation. What we stress on is what we want our listeners to get the meaning from.

Now listen to the audio and listen carefully for the stressed words.

1. They are coming. They are coming.
2. **They** are coming. **They** are coming.

3. They **are** coming. They **are** coming.
4. They are **coming**. They are **coming**.

The stressed words are pronounced:
1. Higher in pitch
2. Longer in vowel length
3. May even be louder

Compare the difference.

They
They
They
They

They are coming.
They are coming.
They are coming.
They are coming.

Again, higher pitch, longer vowel length and may even be louder. Let's compare the difference between the two are's..

Are
Are
Are
Are

They are coming.
They **are** coming.
They are coming.
They **are** coming.

And now the word coming.

Coming
Coming
Coming
Coming

They are coming.
They are **coming**.
They are coming.
They are **coming**.

In the previous four chapters, we have learned
- the dropped vowel sounds
- the reduced vowel sounds
- the regular vowel sounds
- the stressed vowel sounds

These are word intonation. In this chapter, we'll learn sentence intonation. Again, stressed words in sentences are pronounced:
1. Higher in pitch
2. Longer in vowel length
3. May even be louder

Let's practice sentence intonation!

1. Good morning.
2. **Good** morning.
3. Good **morning**.

4. How are you?
5. **How** are you?
6. How **are** you?
7. How are **you**?

8. Fine. Thanks.
9. **Fine**. Thanks.
10. Fine. **Thanks**.

11. Would you like some water?
12. **Would** you like some water?
13. Would **you** like some water?
14. Would you **like** some water?
15. Would you like **some** water?
16. Would you like some **water**?

17. They all have different meanings.
18. **They** all have different meanings.
19. They **all** have different meanings.

20. They all **<u>have</u>** different meanings.
21. They all have **<u>different</u>** meanings.
22. They all have different **<u>meanings</u>**.

Now how do you know what they really mean? Simple.
Listen for the stressed words.

Now let's look at the following.

1. That's a **beautiful** sunset!
2. That's a beautiful sun**rise**!

In the first sentence, the speaker is saying that the sunset is beautiful. The speaker is stressing on the word "beautiful."

In the second sentence, the speaker is correcting the first speaker about the time of the day by stressing on the word *sunrise*. Since both sunset and sunrise have the word *sun* in the beginning, the only part in *sunrise* that needs stress is *rise*.

Let's try that again.

1. That's a **beautiful** sunset!
2. That's a beautiful sun**rise**!

3. That's a **beautiful** sunset!
4. That's a beautiful sun**rise**!

Now try the following.

1. Did you go to the supermarket yesterday?
2. **Yes**, I did.

3. Did you go to the supermarket yesterday?
4. Yes, I went at **seven**.

5. Did you go to the supermarket yesterday?
6. Yes, I went to the **produce** department.

7. Did you go to the supermarket yesterday?
8. Yes, I went to **Starbucks**, too.

9. Did you go to the supermarket yesterday?
10. Yes, milk was **on sale** yesterday!

Let's try them again.

1. Did you go to the supermarket yesterday?
2. **Yes**, I did.

3. Did you go to the supermarket yesterday?
4. Yes, I went at **seven**.

5. Did you go to the supermarket yesterday?
6. Yes, I went to the **produce** department.

7. Did you go to the supermarket yesterday?
8. Yes, I went to **Starbucks**, too.

9. Did you go to the supermarket yesterday?
10. Yes, milk was **on sale** yesterday!

The following sentences are identical, but some of them have the opposite meaning of what they appear to be.

1. That is wonderful.
2. **That** is wonderful.
3. That **is** wonderful.
4. That is **wonderful!**
5. **That** is **wonderful!**

Line 1 is normal. It just tells our listeners that whatever is going on there is wonderful. The whole line is flat. It's an answer to the following question:

Is that wonderful?

That is wonderful.

Line 2 is emphasized on *that*, which is whatever is going on there. *Wonderful* is secondary here. It's an answer to the following question:

What's wonderful?

Line 3, however, is about whether or not whatever is happening is wonderful. It's an answer to the following question:

Is that wonderful or not?

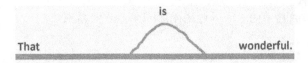

Line 4 is an answer to the following question:

How do you like that?

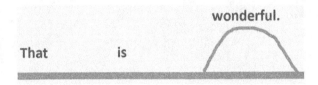

Line 5 is the complete opposite of line 1. Not only it's not praising whatever is going on there is wonderful, its actual meaning is whatever is going on there is not wonderful.

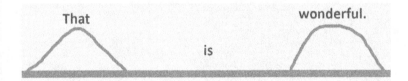

In line 5, imagine this:
1. You bought a new cell phone.
2. You held it on your hand and smiled.
3. You slipped and dropped the phone in the water.

That is when you say "**That** is **wonderful!**"

Now that we have a pair of trained ears. It's easy to find out what the speaker really means. Listen for the stressed words.

In natural speaking, the stressed words are spoken just slightly higher in pitch than the rest of the words, but the vowel is easy to find out.

Again, stressed vowels are pronounced:
1. Higher in pitch
2. Longer in vowel length
3. May even be louder

Chapter 24: Consonant Overview

Other than the five vowels, the rest of the letters are consonants. These consonants can combine with other consonants to form other consonant sounds.

There are two types of consonants, voiced and voiceless.

Put our hand on our throat and say /M/.

Do we feel the vibration on our throat? This is important. Try again until we feel the vibration. Say /MMMMMMMMMM/ longer until we feel the vibration.

We feel the vibration because our vocal cords vibrate on /M/. We called /M/ a voiced consonant.

Now put our hand on our throat and say /S/.

Do we feel any vibration? Say /SSSSSS/ for as long as we can. /S/ is just air flowing out between the gaps of our teeth and our tongue. There is absolutely no vibration.

We feel no vibration because our vocal cords don't vibrate on /S/. We called /S/ a voiceless consonant.

There are only nine voiceless consonants. Keep our hand on our throat and try them.

/CH/, /F/, /H/, /K/, /P/, /S/, /SH/, /T/.

Try them again. Remember, no vibration.

/CH/, /F/, /H/, /K/, /P/, /S/, /SH/, /T/.

Now that we have tried eight of them. There is one more – the sound formed from the letters TH.

TH can be voiced or voiceless. Let's look at the voiceless TH first. Look at this word.

    Thank

    Thank

    Thank

The TH in "thank" is voiceless.

Now let's look at the voiced TH. Look at this word.

    Than

    Than

    Than

The TH in "than" is voiced.

We'll get to these two in details in the later chapters.

Other than the nine voiceless consonants, the rest are voiced consonants. Keep our hand on our throat and say the following. They all have vibration.

/B/, /D/, /G/, /J/, /L/, /M/, /N/, /NG/, /R/, /TH/, /V/, /W/, /Y/, /Z/, /ZH/

Try again. Feel the vibration.

/B/, /D/, /G/, /J/, /L/, /M/, /N/, /NG/, /R/, /TH/, /V/, /W/, /Y/, /Z/, /ZH/

Let's get to each of these consonants in details in the following chapters.

Chapter 25: The B, /B/ and the P, /P/ Sounds

Let's hear the B, /B/ sound first.

Baby, ball, bat, beautiful, bee, Betty, bill, blink, boss, bug, busy.

To pronounce /B/, close our lips. Let me say this again. To pronounce /B/, close *both* of our lips. Quickly part the lips to produce the /B/ sound. Part our lips by sending our upper lip upward and our lower lip downward. Yes. Upper lip up. Lower lip down. There is almost no air coming out as we part our lips this way. Hold a piece of paper in front of our mouth as we say /B/. The paper should stay still.

Put a hand on our throat to feel the vibration. /B/. /B/. /B/. Yes, /B/ is a voiced consonant. Feel the vibration. /B/. /B/. /B/.

Let's practice /B/:

1. /B/ with B in the beginning:
     bag, bagel, bake, baker, ball, bank, base, basil, batch, beach, bean, beige, belief, believe, below, belt, berry, best, bicycle, biker, big, Billy, bin, bird, blender, boat, box, brain, bring, brink, broccoli, buddy, buffalo, build, bush, bite.

2. /B/ with B in the middle:
     Abacus, abbreviation, ability, able, aboard, about, above, abrasive, absent, absolutely, acceptable, accountable, affordable, baboon, baby, Barbara, capability, database, elaborate, establish, fabric, fabulous, gigabyte, habit, label, lullaby, neighborhood, rabbit

3. /B/ with B at the end:
absorb, adverb, barb

When B is at the end, we need to do one extra thing – hold the vowel sound longer before B.

Now let me say that again – hold the vowel sound longer before B.

Let's take "job" as an example. Hold the sound of the letter O longer. Say "Jo—b." "Jo—b."

Now /B/ with B at the end:
absorb, adverb, barb. Did we hold the vowel sound longer before B? Yes? Good job! Let's hold the vowel sounds longer. Bathtub, blob, Bob, bulb cab, club, herb, hub, Jacob, job, knob, lab, rib, Rob, scrub, superb, swab, tab, web

Now let's practice /B/ in sentences.

1. Bag the bagels the baker baked then bring a blank check to the bank.
2. Base on the batch of basil in the basket, it's better to bathe the beans on the beach.
3. I believe your belief is the best. Would you like to beat the drum with balloons?
4. Below the bell peppers are blackberries. Bring big Billy and beautiful Betty to play *Beauty and the Beast*.
5. A bluebird is eating bread. A buffalo is chewing broccoli. Bring your buddy. Let's party.
6. An abacus has the ability to build up numbers. Abigail is able to use the abacus to make money.
7. Welcome aboard. We're about to brush these abrasive stones.
8. Being absent is absolutely acceptable because they're about to divide the money from the table.
9. The baboon is having a baby. Barbara, would you sing her a lullaby and get ready a party?
10. The database is elaborated here. Let's get into a habit of celebrating with a rabbit.
11. Bob likes to absorb adverbs in the bathtub and does a better job than in the lab.
12. Barbara and Bob bought some light bulbs and took the cab to the lab.
13. Jacob has a hub, a job, and a doorknob. He exchanged all of them for a superb swab.

Now let's hear the P, /P/ sound.

Lamp, paint, palm, Paul, peel, person, people, piano, pie, pool, pot, pull, push, python, wasp

When /P/ is in the beginning or at the end of a word, close our lips, build pressure inside our mouth, and quickly part the lips outward to release the pressure. We part our lips by sending our upper lip outward. We part our lips by sending our lower lip outward. Yes. Release our lips and send them outward by the air in the mouth. The pressure will send out a puff of air. Hold a piece of paper in front of our mouth as we say /P/. The puff of air will move the paper.

Let's try it again. /P/, /P/, /P/.

Although the air pressure moves the paper, /P/ is a voiceless consonant. Put the other hand on our throat. There should be no vibration.

Now let's get /P/.

1. /P/ with P in the beginning:
Pace, pad, page, paid, pale, peace, perch, pile, pigeon, pillow, pilot, pioneer, pipeline, pocket, poem, podcast, pointer, popular, portrait, positive, post, powerful, praise, pressure, price, principle, printer, priority, privacy, procedure, produce, product, productivity, professional, professor, program, promise, promotion, proofread, protein, protocol, proud, public, pumpkin, punctuation, pure, push, pyramid.

2. P, /P/ at the end of a word. When /P/ is at the end of a word, it's okay to say /P/ with or without a puff of air.
Asleep, backup, barbershop, buildup, bump, camp, cap, cheap, clap, clip, cleanup, creep, crop, cup, dealership, deep, desktop, develop, drop, dump, fingertip, grip, help, hiccup, hilltop, jump, keep, ketchup, laptop, leadership, lollipop, loop, ownership, Quickstep, relationship, sheep, ship, soap, swap, sweep, trap, trip, top, up, wrap

3. When P, /P/ is in the middle of a word. When /P/ is in the middle of a word, close our lips before /P/, then part the lips and quickly link to the next part of the word. The puff of air is greatly reduced to almost none. Let's take a look at the following word.

Spring

Say /SP/ by holding the puff of air on /P/. Say /S/ and stop the /S/ sound on the letter P like this: /SP/, /SP/, /SP/. Then quickly link to the letter R. /SPR/, /SPR/, /SPR/. SPRing.

Now, the /P/ sound in SPRing is still a different sound than the B, /B/ sound. SPRing is not SBRing. There is no vibration on the letter P.

Let's try /P/ with P in the middle:
Alpine, amplify, appear, appetizer, apple, application, appointment, appreciate, appropriate, approve, capability, capital, captain, caterpillar, competition, compress, copyright, display, employ, empower, episode, expand, experience, expert, expire, explain, express, happen, happy, helpful, hippo, leopard, maple, opportunities, opposite, outperform, spring

Let's practice P, /P/ In sentences.

1. Place the pads piece by piece and page by page until the peace pigeons perch.
2. Pioneer this pipeline project, pal, or put a pillow in the pilot's pocket.
3. Post party pictures on a PowerPoint presentation for the poem podcast then ponder the procedure.
4. Print the popular portrait with positive praises and post powerful promises to give away pumpkins.
5. Praise the professor for her principle when she's under pressure for producing a privacy program.
6. Put the printer price like a pyramid then proofread it.
7. Be proud of your professionalism in the public and put protein in pumpkins in private.
8. Backup when the sheep are asleep, then go to the barbershop and clap.
9. Bump the camp with party balloons then cap the cup deep.
10. Your desktop needs a cleanup. Go to the dealership to get a mop then creep up the hilltop until you hiccup.
11. Develop this crop then drop your laptop.
12. keep the ketchup and swap the lollipop.
13. Grip with your fingers and sweep with your fingertip to show your leadership.
14. Go to the Alpines to amplify your appearance then eat an apple for appetizer.
15. Make an appointment for your application and appreciate the competition.
16. Approve the capability of the caterpillar then employ its power.
17. The captain uses capital letters to compress the copyright display and empowers an expert to write the next episode.
18. Expect to expand your experience by explaining the express map.
19. Helpful hippos and leopards happen to be happy about their opportunities.

Now let's compare the B, /B/ and the P, /P/ sounds.
> Back, pack
> bush, push
> cab, cap

Let's train our ears to hear the slight differences.
   1. Voiced and voiceless.
      /B/, /P/. /B/, /P/.
   2. Longer and shorter vowel lengths.

When saying words with /B/, hold the vowel length longer.

In the word "cap," the vowel length is short. Cap. In the word "cab," the B, /B/, is voiced, the vowel length is longer. Cab. Let's try them again.
> Cap, cab
> Cap, cab
> Cap, cab

Now let's get them.

Back, pack
Bay, pay,
Bass, pace
Batch, patch
beach, peach
bell, pell
berry, Perry
best, pest
bike, pike
big, pig
bin, pin
bush, push

Now let's practice them when they're at the end of a word. Again, for the /B/ sounds, keep the vowel length longer.
Cap, cab
carp, carb
hop, hub

lap, lab
rip, rib
swap, swab
tap, tab

Now let's practice /P/ and /B/ in the same sentences.
1. Bring a backpack to the bay to pay.
2. Base on our pace, we can bring a batch of patch to Peach Beach.
3. Let Perry plow the garden until the berries are buried.
4. Use our bike's pike as the best pest control if we want to lose our big pig.
5. Put the pin in the bin then push the bush.
6. Wear your cap in the cab and call Bob to rub his rabbit.
7. If your hub can hop, put it on your lap and bring it to the lab.
8. Turn on the lamp for your lamb so it won't rip its rib. (The B in lamb is silent)
9. Swap the swab then tap the tab.

Chapter 26: The D, /D/ and the T, /T/ Sounds

Let's hear the D, /D/ sound first.

Dad, daily, dandelion, day, deal, dice, diagram, document, dune, found, good, mode, proud

To pronounce /D/, slightly open our lips, press the tip of our tongue against our teeth and our gum ridge. Release the pressure to produce the /D/ sound. We should feel that we're almost saying the letter N except we release our gum ridge to produce the /D/ sound.

Put a hand on our throat to feel the vibration. /D/. /D/. /D/. Yes, /D/ is a voiced consonant. Feel the vibration. /D/. /D/. /D/.

Now let's practice /D/:

1. When /D/ is at the beginning of a word.
   Daisy, data, December, deep, deer, deliver, dessert, diamond, dinner, dip, direction, disk, do, dock, duck, done, donkey, dusk, duty, dweller

2. When /D/ is in the middle of a word.
   Adapt, adult, audio, edge, edit, idea, identify, index, jade, lander, middle, modern, order, podium, window

3. When /D/ is at the end of a word.
   Just like the letter B, /B/, D, /D/ is also a voiced consonant. When D, /D/ is at the end of a word, we need to do one extra thing – hold the vowel sound before D longer.

Now let me say that again – hold the vowel sound before D longer.

Let's take "food" as an example. Hold the sound of the letters

OO longer. Say "foo—d." "foo—d."

Now when D, /D/ is at the end of a word.
> Add, avoid, bird. Did we hold the vowel sounds longer
> before D? Yes? Good! Let's hold the vowel sounds longer.
> Blend, build, celebrated, could, dated, excited, extend,
> eyelid, find, ground, hood, kid, land, mend, need, odd,
> proud, red, round, solid, Ted, wanted, wind

Now let's practice D, /D/ in sentences.

1. Deer eat daisies in December then sleep in the deep forest.
2. Deliver a dessert in the desert and do a Donkey Dance.
3. Dine at Diner for dinner and pay the dinner with dimes.
4. Dim the lights at dusk and dance until dawn.
5. Adjust to the speed of sound then listen to the recordings of hounds.
6. The recording of the audio is done. That's it for today. Let's go to lunch.
7. Can you identify diamonds and jades? They look identical to me.
8. Edit the index in the middle of the window then order a modern pillow.
9. Add a podium in the middle of the stadium to build up the crowd. Avoid birds flying around.
10. Celebrated with orange smoothies on hand, the students were excited to get a diploma again.
11. Extend your hand to a new friend. Find a common ground to sit down.
12. Land on the red planet to study the land. There are strong winds there and the atmosphere is not dense.

Now let's feel the T, /T/ sound.

Ate, best, chat, dent, elite, fast, get, take, talk, taught, tilt, tutor, type.

To pronounce /T/, slightly open our lips, press the tip of our tongue against our teeth to build tension. Release the tension to produce the sound. /T/. /T/. /T/.

/T/ is one of the voiceless sounds. Now put a hand on your throat. Do you feel any vibration when saying /T/? Your vocal cords are not vibrated at all. There should absolutely be no vibration. Keep trying until you get it right. /T/, /T/, /T/.

Let's practice /T/.

1. When /T/ is in the beginning: Tablet, tackle, tag, tail, take, tall, tango, tea, technology, tell, temperature, tennis, terrific, test, text, ticket, tide, Tiffany, tiger, tight, tilt, time, tip, tissue, twinkle, toad, token, Tommy, took, torch, tough, tube, tunnel, turn, typhoon
2. When /T/ is at the end: appointment, at, attract, copyright, attempt, default, decent, dessert, detect, detergent, expect, fast, fruit, hat, intact, intelligent, interest, invent, it, kit, light, might, paint, put, request, rest, sit, talent

When /T/ is in the middle of a word, hold the pressure on the letter T, then release the pressure and quickly link to the next part of the word. Let's take a look at the following word.

Step

Say /ST/ by holding the pressure on /T/. Say /S/ and stop the /S/ sound on the letter T like this: /ST/, /ST/, /ST/. Then quickly link to the letter E. /STep/, /STep/, /STep/.

Now, the /T/ sound is still a different sound than the /D/ sound. STep is not SDep. The letter T is free of vibration.

3. Now let's practice /T/ when /T/ is in the middle:
   Atmosphere, attach, attend, attitude, automatic, capital,
   captain, caterpillar, competition, detail, extension,
   gatekeeper, intention, integrity, internal, international,
   interesting, inventor, outperform, outstanding, stamp, steep,
   stick, student

Let's practice /T/ in sentences.
1. Tap on the tablet to tackle the task.
2. Technology makes taking tests terrific. Students send texts while taking tests.
3. Today's temperature is perfect to play tennis. Tie your tiger while playing tennis with your brother.
4. Tommy has two tokens. Tammy has two tickets. Bring a torch and let's catch some crickets.
5. Time to turn right into the tunnel and watch the tornado.
6. At an attempt to attract a decent expert, bring some dessert.
7. To detect the detergent, wear a helmet. Expect a fast result, switch to a hat.
8. Building up his interest to invent an intelligent kit, Ted went to the desert and built a fire pit.
9. To wet your bed, go to the left. To tie your tie, go the right.
10. Sit on the beach and light up a light then harness your talent through the night.
11. In its tight atmosphere, Venus welcomes competition.
12. To attend the party bring a tent. Kids like to count to ten.
13. With a tough attitude in extent, bring more capital to spend.
14. The Captain Caterpillar Competition goes automatic. Invite a guest to take a peek.
15. Integrity is an outstanding character. Persistent inventors are welcome to drink water.

Now let's compare D, /D/ and T, /T/.

First, let's compare them when D and T are in the beginning or in the middle.

dab, tab
dag, tag
deer, tear
dense, tense
dime, time
dip, tip
do, to
dock, tock
done, ton
dune, tune
dusk, tusk

Now let's practice them when D and T are at the end. Their differences are:

1. Vibration. No vibration.
2. Longer vowel length. Shorter vowel length.

Let's try them first.
ad, at
bid, bit,
build, built

When pronouncing words with D, /D/, hold the vowel length longer.

Again, for the D, /D/ sounds, feel the vibration and keep the vowel length longer.

ad, at
bid, bit,
build, built
extend, extent
feed, feet

hid, hit
kid, kit
lid, lit
ladder, latter
mid, Mitt
nod, not
pod, pot
rod, rot
wed, wet

Now let's take a look at the following. See if we can tell any difference between the ending sounds.

cabbed, capped
served, surfed
bagged, backed

These three pairs all have different ending sounds. The first words have the D, /D/ ending sound. The second words have the T, /T/ ending sound.

Remember the voiceless consonants? Here they are again: /CH/, /F/, /H/, /K/, /P/, /S/, /SH/, /T/, /TH/. When these voiceless consonants are in front of the ED ending, then ED has the T, /T/ sound. Other than in front of these voiceless consonants, the ED endings will end up to be in front of the voiced consonants which have the D, /D/ sound.

Let's hear these three again!

cabbed, capped
served, surfed
bagged, backed

Do we understand this? Yes? Good! Let's continue for more.

bobbed, bopped
ribbed, ripped
tabbed, tapped
carved, scarfed
proved, proofed
waived, waifed
bugged, bucked
chugged, chucked
clogged, clocked
logged, locked
sagged, sacked
slagged, slacked

Good job! We are almost there. Now look at these two pairs.

braised, braced
closed, crossed

Note that in braised and closed, there is one S in front of ED. The S in these words is pronounced as Z, /Z/. There is a vibration on /Z/. Therefore ED in these words is pronounced as D, /D/. However, when a verb ends with double S, the double S is pronounced as S, /S/. Therefore, ED is pronounced as T, /T/. Also in BRACED, CE is pronounced as S, /S/ Therefore, ED is also pronounced as T, /T/.

Let's hear them again!

braised, braced
closed, crossed

Let's continue for more.

cruised
eased
discussed
guessed
passed
processed

Now the last one before we get to the easiest one. Words with CH, /CH/ and SH, /SH/ sounds.

Approached
bleached
cached
crunched
watched
accomplished
finished
polished

pushed
washed

Remember the voiceless consonants? CH, /CH/ and SH, /SH/ are among them. When these voiceless consonants are in front of the ED ending, then ED has the T, /T/ sound.

This is an easy one. Let's perfect them now. What should we do? Repeat after me! Every time! Throughout the book! Repeat my instructions, too. Ready, steady, spaghetti, Go!

Approached
bleached
cached
crunched
watched
accomplished
finished
polished
pushed
washed

Now the easiest one:

Attended, loaded, printed, vented

For these words that end with D or T, we add an extra vowel sound at the end. Otherwise, they would have sounded like "attend'd, load'd, print't, and so forth. What do we do? Add an extra vowel sound at the end. Here are more of them. Let's get them.

Added
concluded
divided
exceeded
melted
painted
tilted

vented

Remember the voiceless consonants? T, /T/ is one of the voiceless consonants. When these voiceless consonant are in front of the ED ending, then ED has the T, /T/ sound. What about D, /D/? D, /D/ is voiced. Therefore, the ED endings after D, /D/ will end up to be having the D, /D/ sound.

Let's hear them again.

Added
concluded
divided
exceeded
melted
painted
tilted
vented

Hooray! We've done it!

Chapter 27: The F, /F/, the V, /V/, and the W, /W/ Sounds

Let's first hear the /F/ sound.

Face, fact, fly, fierce, fifteen, fruit, fun, itself

To pronounce the /F/ sound, slightly touch our lower lip with our upper teeth, keep that position and let the air flow out slowly between the gaps.

Now ask ourselves this: Is /F/ voiced or voiceless?

Right! It's voiceless. The /F/ sound can be formed from the letters F and PH. Let's practice /F/:

1. When /F/ is in the beginning of a word.
   Fable, faded, fare, feel, feed, feast, find, flight, flounder, flower, focus, food, found, Frank, frost, full, fun, Philadelphia, Philips, physics, physician,
2. When /F/ is in the middle of a word.
   Alpha, buffalo, beautiful, different, fifteen, fluffy, gift, left, loft, office, raft, reference, safe, sofa, Sophia, traffic, wafer, waffle, wife, wonderful
3. When /F/ is at the end of a word.
   Behalf, belief, chief, cliff, golf, half, herself, laugh, liftoff, payoff, proof, scarf, sniff, staff, stuff, wolf

Now let's practice /F/ in sentences.

1. Anderson's fables haven't faded with time. Pay a fare to bring a pair.
2. Feed this beast a feast before finding it a flight or a kite.
3. Is it a flounder or a flower? You can find out if you focus on the formula.
4. Frank is full of fun. Phil is full at lunch.
5. When the alpha buffalo arrived, the fifteen different chiefs laughed.
6. Bring this fluffy gift to the office, and take the raft home.
7. To help Sophia become a terrific wife, bring her flowers and waffles.
8. Refresh my memory, tell me a brief story.
9. Half of the staff went to California. The other half stayed to prepare for other stuff.

Now let's hear the V, /V/ sound.

Above, achieve, believe, carve, hover, positive, very, victory

To pronounce V, /V/, slightly touch our lower lip with our upper teeth, keep that position and gently force the air out <u>with vibration.</u>

Does V, /V/ sound the same as F, /F/? Listen again.
/V/, /F/.
/V/, /F/.

They sound almost the same, but they are different.

For the V, /V/, put a hand on our throat to feel the vibration. It's just a little vibration, but we've got to feel it.
/V/
/V/
/V/
Keep trying until we feel the little vibration. /V/. /V/. /V/.

For F, /F/, simply let the air out. For V, /V/, use our belly muscle to help force the air up. Tighten our belly and push the air up with vibration. /V/. /V/. /V/.

Let's practice the V, /V/ sound:

1. When V, /V/ is at the beginning of a word.
   Vacation, vacuum, valid, value, vapor, vast, vein, vendor, ventilation, very, Victoria, video, view, voiced, volleyball, volume, vowel, voyage,

2. When V, /V/ is in the middle of a word.
   Advantage, civilization, cover, development, driver, envelope, given, lava, level, movie, navigator, novel, November, pivotal, review, river, seventeen, travel

3. When V, /V/ is at the end of a word.
   Abrasive

achieve
alternative
positive

When V, /V/ is at the end of a word. we need to do one extra thing – hold the vowel sound before V longer.

Let's take "achieve" as an example. Hold the sound of the letters IE longer. Say "achie—v." "achie—v."

3. When V, /V/ is at the end:
Abrasive, achieve, alternative, attractive, believe, cave, conducive, creative, decisive, five, live, productive, shave, twelve, wave

Let's practice V, /V/ in sentences.

1. Take a vacation, visit the Vatican. Take an eating tour, go to Vancouver.
2. To voyage through the vacuum of space, a valid vendor's verification is valuable.
3. Turn up the volume very high if you want to hear the voiceless consonants and the voice of grapevines.
4. Scientists believe advanced civilizations had developed on vast regions of Earth in the past.
5. Lava has covered the river. Feel free to drive across in November.
6. Very successful people do three things – they eat, they breathe, and they achieve.
7. To be creative, be decisive.
8. Live in caves to be productive. What an alternative!
9. Wave at twelve then shave at five. He's investing in a new life.

Now let's compare the /F/ and /V/ sounds.

fan, van
favor, vapor
fast, vast
fender, vendor
ferry, very
few, view
fine, vine

Now look at these three pairs.

Belief, believe
life, live
proof, prove

There are two differences in these three pairs.
1. Voiced and voiceless.
2. Longer and shorter vowel lengths.

V, /V/ is voiced. When saying words with V, /V/, hold the vowel length longer.

Let's try them again!
Belief, believe
Fife, five
half, have
leaf, leave
life, live
proof, prove

Now let's hear the W, /W/ sound.

Always, anywhere, awake, biweekly, rewind, swan, swim, twelve, was, wet, window, work

Let's first hear the W, /W/ sound and the V, /V/ sound.
/W/, /V/.
/W/, /V/.

Does /W/ sound the same as /V/? /W/ is a completely different sound than the /V/ sound. Let's get it right.

To pronounce W, /W/, slightly round our lips, tighten our belly muscles to force the air out, and add vibration. /W/. /W/. Our lips are rounded and extended forward while our <u>teeth are away</u> from our lips.

Put a hand on our throat to feel the vibration. Put a piece of paper in front of our mouth to see the air flow. /W/. /W/. The flowing air should be strong enough to move the paper.

For F, /F/, touch our lower lip with our upper teeth and slowly let the air out between the gaps. /F/. For V, /V/, touch our lower lip with our upper teeth, vibrate, and tighten our belly to slowly push the air up and out between our teeth and our lips. /V/. /V/. For W, /W/, also tighten our belly to push the air up. Our lips are rounded and extended forward while our teeth are away from our lips. /W/. /W/.

Let's practice the W, /W/ sound:

1. When W, /W/ is in front of a word.
    Wagon, walk, wallpaper, want, water, wave, went, wheel, whistle, wilderness, windmill, within, why, whisper, wonderful, workshop, woodchuck

2. When W, /W/ is in the middle of a word.
    always, awaken, award, awhile, between, dishwasher, likewise, overwhelming, password, runway, swab,

swallow, swamp, swear, sweet, sweeper, swerve, swipe, switch, swim, tweak, twelve, twilight, twin

3. When W, /W/ is at the end of a word.
   When W, is at the end of a word, W becomes part of a vowel. Here is a good example, in the word pillow, the W is part of the /OH/ sound.

Now let's practice the W, /W/ in sentences.
1. Walk to the wagon then ride to the water or pull the wagon and walk to the water.
2. Whistling in the wilderness will scare the shrew. Whispering in the workshop and no one will hear you.
3. The awakened gets the reward. The sleeping barely gets any water.
4. Do you want to see a swan swimming in the swamp or a swallow sweeping pass the willow?
5. Always wake up the sweepers at twilight and then swallow a sweet potato.
6. Swipe a tiger you'd better hide. Tigers are sized to fight worldwide.

Now let's compare W, /W/ and V, /V/.
wallet, valid
wan, van
Wayne, vein
ways, vase
went, vent
wary, vary
whale, vail
wheel, veal
wine, vine
while, vial
wiper, viper
wise, vice
wiser, visor
word, verb
wow, vow

What is he driving? A wan or a van?
He is driving a van.

Chapter 28: The G, /G/ and the K, /K/ Sounds

Let's hear the G, /G/ sound.

Agree, begin, big, dragonfly, gap, get, gift, good, glider, gold, magnet, Oregon, zigzag

To pronounce the G, /G/ sound, slightly open our lips, press the back of our tongue up against the roof of our mouth then release the pressure to produce the sound. /G/. Put a hand on our throat to feel the vibration.

Let's practice the G, /G/ sound:

1. When G, /G/ is in the front:
   Gain, girl, glad, gallon, garlic, gaze, gear, gigabyte, glance, glove, glow, gorilla, gap, grass, gravity, great, green, guitar

2. When G, /G/ is in the middle:
   Again, ago, agree, alligator, cargo, eager, egg, elegant, figure, giggle, Google, igloo, ignite, ignore, juggle, logo, magnify, sugar, tiger, toggle, trigger

3. When G, /G/ is at the end:
   bag
   big
   brag

When G, /G/ is at the end of a word, we need to do one extra thing – hold the vowel sound before G longer.

Again, hold the vowel sound before G longer.

Let's take "bag" as an example. Hold the sound of the letter A longer. Say "ba—g." "ba—g."

Now when G, /G/ is at the end:

bag, big, brag, bug, catalog, clog, dialog, dog, drag, egg, fig, firebug, flag, frog, hedgehog, iceberg, leapfrog, leg, plug, polliwog, prologue, stag, tag, twig, zigzag

Now let's practice G, /G/ in sentences.

1. The girl grabbed a guitar then played to a gorilla.
2. To lead our horse to green grass, stay away from the glacier.
3. Who runs faster, a gopher or a grasshopper?
4. What a wonder! A tiger racing an alligator.
5. An eagle flew over the jungle a minute ago. Did you get any photos?
6. Bag this big bug and put it in the backpack. Release the big bug to see if our dog will clap.
7. Is it a leapfrog or a polliwog on the catalog?
8. The frog, the dog, and the hog, jumped into the water to fetch the log.

Now let's hear the K, /K/ sound.

Ask, bake, book, buckle, chalk, keep, key, kindle, kite, like, maker, mark, package, rock

To pronounce the K, /K/ sound, slightly open our lips, press the back of our tongue up against the roof of our mouth then quickly release the pressure to let the air out. Put a hand on our throat. /K/ is a voiceless sound. There is no vibration.

The /K/ sound can be formed from the letters K, C, and QU.

1. When /K/ is in the beginning of a word.
    khaki, kangaroo, kayak, keel, keen, keep, keepsake, ketchup, keyboard, kickoff, kick-start, kid, kilogram, kilometer, kind, kinetic, king, kit, kitchen, kite, kiwi

2. The letter C is pronounced as /K/ when it's in front of the letters A, U, L, R, and T.
    cab, cable, call, camera, canal, candy, captain, car, careful, carpet, carrot, catch, class, clean, climb, clue, coach, color, comfortable, craft, crew, culture, customer, cute, exact

3. When /K/ is in the middle of a word.
    ankle, accomplish, account, accurate, action, awaken, baker, echo, hiker, hockey, liken, likewise, maker, poker, scarf, scatter, school, scoop, skate, ski, skill, skim, skip, skirt, sky, sprinkle, token, walker

4. When /K/ is in at the end of a word.
    arc, automatic, basic, civic, classic, disc, generic, italic, kinetic, logic, magic, magnetic, music, organic, Pacific, public, terrific topic, ask, book, click, clock, desk, duck, elk, hammock, look, neck, speak, talk, thank, think, track

5. The letters QU are pronounced as /K/ and sometimes /KW/.
    equipment, liquid, mosquito, quack, quad, quadrant,

quadruple, quake, quality, quarter, queue, queen, quick, quiet, quilts, quite, quiz, quote, request, require, sequence, squash, squeeze, squirrel

Let's practice /K/ in sentences.
1. Have you seen a khaki kangaroo kayaking a kilometer?
2. Keep the keyboard as a keepsake and kick the ketchup as a kick-start.
3. Was it a car or a cat I saw?
4. Call a cab and pay with candy then give the driver cash.
5. Catch the carrot with a carpet. If you have no clue on how, bow.
6. Acknowledged. Take actions to accomplish.
7. This account is accurate. Wake up the baker and the hiker to play poker.
8. Students scatter at school to play scooter.
9. The basic disc is automatic.
10. This magic is basic logic. Put on music to show the public.
11. Ask a book for an answer and you can wait for the clock to tick.
12. Teach a duck to use the hammock and you can expect to hear it quack.
13. Mosquitoes drink liquid. Quails and ducks walk.
14. Quality or quantity, which did you pick? The sun is more significant than a million stars.

Now let's compare /G/ and /K/.

gap, cap
gable, cable
glass, class
glean, clean
glue, clue

Now look at these three pairs.

Bag, back
plug, pluck
tag, tack

There are two differences.
1. Voiced and voiceless.
2. Longer and shorter vowel lengths.

/G/ is voiced. When pronouncing words with /G/, hold the vowel length longer. Let's get them right.

clog, clock
bag, back
beg, beck
big, Bick
bug, buck
dog, dock
dug, duck
flag, flack
plug, pluck
rag, rack
stag, stack
tag, tack

Now Let's look these words:
accomplish, account, economy, incorporated,

In these words, the syllables with the /K/ sounds are stressed. They are pronounced with higher pitch than the rest of the syllables. Let's hear them again.

accomplish, accounT, economy, incorporated,

In these words, the letter C, /K/ has the regular /K/ sound.

Now let's look at the following words:
ankle, accurate, awaken

In these words, however, the syllables with the /K/ sounds are not stressed. Some other syllables are pronounced with higher pitch than the syllables with the /K/ sound.

Let's hear them again.
ankle, accurate, awaken

In these words, hold the pressure on the /K/ sound, then release the pressure and quickly link to the next part of the word. Let's take a look at the following word.

Skip

Say /SK/ by holding the pressure on /K/. Say /S/ and stop the /S/ sound on the letter K like this: /SK/, /SK/, /SK/. Then quickly link to the letter i. /SKip/, /SKip/, /SKip/.

Now, the /K/ sound in SKip is a different sound than the /G/ sound. SKip is not SGip. There is no vibration on the letter K. Let's try it.

baker, diskette, echo, gasket, hiker, hockey, husky, liken, duckling, kickoff, risky, sprinkle, whisker,

Chapter 29: The H, /H/ Sound

Let's hear the /H/ sound.

ha, ahead, anthill, handle, happy, harvest, have, hummingbird

To pronounce /H/, warm our hands. In the winter when our hands are cold, we blow warm air to warm our hands. /H/. This time, warm our hands just a little bit. /H/. That's it.

Is /H/ voiced or voiceless? Put a hand on our throat to see if we can feel any vibration. If we feel no vibration, then we've got it right.

/H/ is voiceless. Let's practice /H/:

> ha, hair, hand, hawk, hike, hill, hobby, harmony, helpful, hello, hollow, humor, Harry, habit, hammer, hidden, hockey, hoist, ahead, behold, behalf, behavior, behind, coherent, rehearse, uphill, vehicle

Now let's practice /H/ in sentences.

1. Hello, Harry. What's your hobby?
2. Will you be happy to see humanity living in harmony?
3. Which is more helpful, changing a habit or hiking a mountain?
4. Which is easier, changing a habit or moving a mountain?

Chapter 30: The L, /L/ and the R, /R/ Sounds

Let's hear the L, /L/ sound first.

label, landmark, laughter, lily, license, logical, believe, dollar, elongated, fulfill, helpful

There are two L, /L/ sounds to pronounce.
1. When L, /L/ is in the beginning or in the middle.
2. When L, /L/ is at the end.

First, let's learn the L, /L/ sound when L is in the beginning or in the middle of a word. Touch our upper gum ridge *and* our upper teeth with the tip of our tongue then release the tongue to produce the sound. /L/. /L/. Say Lela. That's where our tongue position should be.

Let's practice L, /L/.

1. When L is in the beginning or in the middle.
   lady, lagoon, lamp, landmark, laughter, lead, leave, led, leg, lift, light, lighthouse, lily, license, long, look, lotus, love, alignment, balloon, believe, beloved, below, Billy, challenger, college, color, dollar, elongated, enlarge, hello, hilarious, hollow, pilot, pillow, splendid, voiceless

When L is at the end of a word, touch our upper gum ridge *behind* our upper teeth with the tip of our tongue and hold it there. Hold it there and hold the /L/ sound long! Let's try the long L sound now.
   Well
   Well
   Well
   I feel well.

Did we hold the L sound long? Let's do it again.

Well
Well
Well
I feel well.

Now let's practice the /L/ sound when L is at the end.
Remember, hold the /L/ sound long.

call, channel, crawl, facial, feel, focal, formal, fulfill,
full, hall, handful, helpful, howl, identical, jewel, label,
logical, middle, normal, pencil, professional, school,
several, social, squirrel, swivel, symbol, tell, thankful,
tunnel, wall

Now let's compare the *extremely* similar sounds with and without L.

The second word is the word with the L sound.

Boat, Bold
Coat, Colt
Doe, Dole

Did we hear the /L/ sound in the second words? On the second words, make sure we pull our tongue up to touch our upper gum ridge *behind* our upper teeth with the tip of our tongue and hold it there. Let's try them again.

Boat, Bold
Coat, Colt
Doe, Dole
Due, Dual
Echo, Equal
Foe, Foal
Go, Goal
How, Howl
Joe, Joel
Mow, Mole
Row, Roll
Sow, Sole
Woe, Wool

Now let's practice L, /L/ in sentences.

1. Look at the ladies at the lagoon! Give them a pencil and a balloon.
2. This lamp is a landmark.
3. Laugh as light as you can!
4. Lead a horse to water and push its head to drink. No matter how strong we are, it's up to the horse to drink.
5. Is it a lotus or a waterlily? Ask Billy if you're silly.
6. What do you call these creepy-crawlies?
7. Feel the energy and fill the void. Focus on one point.
8. These two squirrels look identical. We should give them a label.
9. A candle is helpful. A lamp is thankful. Look! There are jewels on the table!

Now let's hear the R, /R/ sound.

alright, arrive, door, her, more, rather, read, red, real

To pronounce /R/, slightly curl our tongue, bring it up to almost touching the roof of our mouth, and then pull it back down as we push the air out to produce the sound. /R/. /R/. /R/.

Let's practice R, /R/.
1. When R, /R/ is at the beginning of a word.
>   Rabbit, racer, radio, raft, rail, railroad, rain, raisin, rare, read, real, receive, red, reference, referral, refund, renew, rental, repeat, return, review, rhythm, rim, risk, roar, roof, roommate, round, run

2. When R, /R/ is in the middle of a word.
>   Approach, area, around, array, arrive, brake, branch, breakfast, breeze, brief, bright, bring, camera, carrot, compress, crack, crawl, cricket, fresh, front, fruit, grade, grasshopper, interesting, praise, produce, product, proof, truck

3. When R, /R/ is at the end of a word. When R, /R/ is at the end of a word, add an "ER" sound.
>   Advisor, alligator, before, better, biker, car, cheer, color, dear, finger, hair, harbor, honor, humor, silver, sugar, super, sure, tailor, Voyager, winner, wiper, wonder

Let's practice R, /R/ in sentences.

1. Is it a rabbit or a racer on the railroad?
2. Who's going to win the race between the turtle and the hare?
3. Traffic is very different than the traffic report.
4. That's because the traffic report you heard wasn't a real-time traffic report. It was yesterday's traffic report.
5. Renew our book rentals repeatedly and return them to receive a review.
6. To get our raffle tickets, raft in the rain while reading a real story.
7. Run our own risk. Roar at the tiger.
8. When approaching an area around a strange neighborhood, be sure to bring a camera and a carrot.
9. Alligators can be our advisor because alligators can use their fingers better.
10. Super! What an honor! Bring some sugar and some humor, and you're a winner.

Now let's compare the L, /L/ and the R, /R/ sounds.

led, red
lace, race
laser, racer
lane, rain
limb, rim
blink, brink
flesh, fresh
glass, grass
lamp, ramp
light, right
look, rook

What's the only way to get our pronunciation right? Practice!
Let's continue!

all, or
ball, bar
call, car
deal, dear
eel, ear
feel, fear
hail, hair
heel, hear
label, labor
mall, mar
Neal, near
Paul, pour
shall, share
tall, tore

Chapter 31: The M, /M/, N, /N/, and NG, /ŋ/ Sounds

Let's hear the M, /M/ sound.

Memory, most, mystery, semester, system, team, yam

To pronounce /M/, close our lips and let the air flow out from our nose. /M/. /M/. /M/.

Put a hand on our throat. All /M/, /N/, and /ŋ/ sounds are voiced. Feel the vibration.

Let's practice M, /M/:

1. When M, /M/ is in the beginning of a word.
   mace, machine, magazine, magic, magnet, magnify, mailbox, mammal, man, many, map, maple, Mars, mastermind, math, maybe, meditate, mentor, Mercury, milk, mirror, mud, muscle, must

2. When M, /M/ is in the middle of a word.
   Amazing, ambition, amount, amuse, camel, camera, comet, comfortable, amble, emphasize, empty, imbibe, immune, important, improve, optimistic, smart, smile, smooth, summer, tomato

3. When M, /M/ is in at the end of a word.
   Aim, alarm, arm, broom, calcium, charm, claim, confirm, dim, film, gem, inform, rhythm, sum, swim, system, team, term, them, warm, worm

Now let's practice M, /M/ in sentences.

1. Magnify! What's that on the twenty-mile high mountain on Mars? Can you identify?
2. Man! How many maple trees are there on the map? You can do the math.
3. What's on our face, mud or a mustache?
4. Do we make mistakes sometime in life?
5. What a dumb question. If we're a breathing human, we will make mistakes.
6. The camel's back looks comfortable. Especially with the extra humps of muscle.
7. Follow the rhythm, confirm, and watch a film.

Now let's hear the N, /N/ sound.

Attend, interesting, native, natural, pan, typhoon, when

To pronounce /N/, open our lips but raise our tongue up to the roof of our mouth and at the same time touch the teeth to seal the air flow. Although our lips are open, air flows out from our nose. /N/. /N/. /N/.

Let's practice N, /N/.
1. When N, /N/ is in the beginning of a word.
Name, nap, narrow, nation, natural, nature, navigate, need, negotiate, nerve, nest, network, news, next, nice, nickel, Nicole, noodle, normal, north, nose, notebook, notice, noun, novel, now, number, nutrition

2. When N, /N/ is in the middle of a word.
Ana, ancient, animal, antenna, ants, enclose, end, energy, engineer, enjoy, enormous, enroll, entrance, income, indeed, influence, ingredient, instead, intend, interesting, inventor, once, snack, snow, Tiffany, unit, unite

3. When N, /N/ is in at the end of a word.
Action, alien, balloon, begin, between, bin, born, brain, can, captain, children, clean, fan, foreign, Ken, lagoon, learn, lion, moon, ocean, often, oven, plane, pumpkin, ripen, soon, spoon, teen, win

Let's practice N, /N/ in sentences.

1. Take a nap in nature and wake up at night. Eat some noodles then fly a kite.

2. Navigate through the woods to find the bird's nest. Use the North Stars to our best.

3. Ana is the anchor of the Ancient Animal's Channel.

4. Nicole pays with only nickels.

5. Nathan was writing a novel on a notebook when he noticed a fly that landed on his nose.

6. Ants use their antennae to communicate.

7. Engineers enjoy an enormous amount of energy at the entrance.

8. Guess what Ken likes and wants to ride on? A hot air balloon? Noooo. A plane? Noooo. It's a UFO!

9. Children take weird actions when they encounter aliens.

10. If our accent sounds foreign, practice in the ocean.

11. Clean our oven often if we want to take it to the moon.

Now let's get familiar with the, /ŋ/ sound.

Along, anchor, belong, blanket, bring, flamingo, jingle, tango

To pronounce /ŋ/, open our lips but raise our tongue to the middle of our mouth without touching anything. Our mouth is open with nothing blocking the air flow, however, all air flows out from our nose. /ŋ/. /ŋ/. /ŋ/.

Let's practice /ŋ/.

1. When /ŋ/ is at the end of a word. It's formed with NG.
   Along, among, belong, boomerang, bring, clang, cling, clung, hang, king, long, lung, mustang, parking, ring, sing, slang, sting, strong, strung, swing, swung, thing, thong, tongue, wing, young

2. When /ŋ/ is in the middle of a word.
   Belonging, bringing, clinging, hanging, ringing, singing, swinging

3. When /ŋ/ is in the beginning of a word.
   There are none. If we see a word that begins with NG, it's not English.

4. The /ŋ/ sound can also be pronounced as /ŋ/ + G, /ŋG/.
   Angle, entangle, finger, hunger, jingle, jungle, linger, longer, mango, rectangle, singer, single, stronger, tango, triangle

5. The /ŋ/ sound can also be pronounced as /ŋ/ + K, /ŋK/.
   Anchor, anxious, blanket, crank, drink, frank, handkerchief, ink, junk, monkey, rink, thank, think, uncle

Let's practice /ŋ/ in sentences.

1. Bring our boomerang along and place it to where it belongs.

2. Drive a Mustang and use slang.

3. If you have wings, sing, think, and swing.

4. Is it a triangle or a rectangle? Why does it look like a flamingo?

5. If you're single, bring a jingle and a mango. Let the singles tango in the jungle.

6. Frank went to the bank with a blanket in his hand.

7. What do you think about this ink? Mix it with our drink. That would be interesting.

Now let's compare the /M/ /N/, and /ŋ/ sounds.

clan, clam, clang
Dan, dam, dang
din, dim, ding
dun, dumb, dunk
kin, Kim, king
Lynn, limb, ling
ran, ram, rang
run, rum, rung
sin, SIM, sing
sun, sum, sung

Chapter 32: The S, /S/ and the Z, /Z/ Sounds

Let's hear the S, /S/ sound.

Construction, glass, description, floss, ice, impetus, inspiration, sage

To pronounce /S/, slightly open our lips. Press the tip of our tongue against our lower front teeth. Air flows out from the middle part of our tongue through the gaps of our teeth. /S/. /S/. /S/.

Place a hand on our throat. Do we feel any vibration?

Right. /S/ is voiceless. It's just air flowing out through the gaps of our teeth. There is no vibration.

The /S/ sound can be formed from the letters S and C. When the letter C is in front of the vowels E, I, and Y, then C is pronounced as /S/. Let's try some of them.

Celebrate, century, certificate, accelerate

Advice, circle, circus, city, civilization, decide, exercise, face, voice

Bicycle, cylinder, fancy, mercy, recycle

Let's practice /S/:

1. When S, /S/ is in the beginning of a word.
    Satisfy, save, say, sea, send, service, seventeen, silver, simple, singing, six, skate, skill, sky, so, sofa, some, song, space, spider, spike, spring, stay, step, story, sunny, swab, swan

2. When S, /S/ is in the middle of a word.

Absorb, acid, Alisa, ascent, ask, asleep, aspire,
assign, assist, best, blossom, diskette, dust, essay,
essence, grasshopper, guest, husband, insist, inspire,
intensity, just, most, music, must, past, post, reset,
risk

3. When S, /S/ is at the end of a word. Also, the letter C is
pronounced as /S/ when C is in front of the letters E, I and Y.
Address, analysis, bonus, boss, brass, bus, chess,
class, cross, delicious, dress, eclipse, emphasis,
fabulous, famous, floss, ice, impetus, juice, notice,
obsess, office, pass, possess, practice, process,
promise, serious, success, thesis, voice

Remember the voiceless consonants? When a voiceless
consonant is in front of the letter S, then S is pronounced
as /S/. That's right. When the following voiceless consonants

/F/, /K/, /P/, /S/, /T/, /TH/

are in front of the letter S, then the letter S is pronounced
as /S/. In the following words, the letter S is at the end. They
all have the /S/ sound.

academics, logistics, systematics, briefs, kickoffs,
golfs, banks, checks, parks, ships, beeps, caps,
groups, chess, class, success, dusts, guests, posts,
sixteenths

When the letter S is followed by yet another S, then the
double S is pronounced as /S/. Here they are.

Chess, class, glass, success, guess, address, boss,
brass, pass, possess, process, hiss, press, miss,
Mississippi, express, business

Now when the other voiceless consonants, the CH and SH, are in
front of the letter S, the letter S is pronounced as Z, /Z/.
That's because they add a new syllable IZ to the sound.

Let's hear them.
1. approaches, beaches, roaches, brushes, finishes, splashes

Let's get right to the Z, /Z/ sound.

citizen, magazine, size, surprise, user, waltz, whizz, zoo

To pronounce the Z, /Z/ sound, slightly open our lips. Press the tip of our tongue against our lower front teeth. Air flows out from the middle part of our tongue through the gaps of our teeth. This time, add vibration. /Z/, /Z/, /Z/.

Let's try the Z, /Z/ sound.

1. When Z, /Z/ is in the beginning of a word.
zap, zeal, zebra, zucchini, zero, zig, zigzag, zillion, zip, zipper, zither, zombie, zone, zoo, zookeeper, zounds

2. When Z, /Z/ is in the middle of a word.
amazement, azimuth, azure, bizarre, blizzard, citizen, dazzle, dizzy, enzyme, fuzzy, gazer, gazillion, hazel, lizard, magazine, nozzle, ozone, puzzle, razors, sizable, wizard

3. When Z, /Z/ is at the end of a word.
amaze, analyze, apologize, braze, breeze, buzz, emphasize, energize, fuzz, harmonize, hertz, internationalize, jazz, localize, maximize, mobilize, normalize, notarize, personalize, prize, quiz

4. The letter S can also be pronounced as Z, /Z/. Did I say the letter S can also be pronounced as Z, /Z/? Yes, I did. Let's hear it.
Because, choose, compose, does, ease, excuse, hers, his, muse, nose, pause, phrase, please, raise, rinse, surprise, use, user, whose

The letter S in some words can also be pronounced as S, /S/ or Z, /Z/. Let's take a look at the word excuse in the following two sentences. When the word excuse is used as a verb, the

S is pronounced as Z, /Z/. When it's used as a noun, the S is pronounced as S, /S/.

- Excuse me. Where is the gate?
- There is no excuse.

Here are more.
Noun – a houSe, verb – to houZe the new arrivals.
Noun – a cloSe, verb – to cloZe the door.

Let's practice them. The first one is a noun. The second one is a verb.

Excuse, Excuse
House, House
Close, Close
Use, Use
Mouse, Mouse
Advice, Advise

Now let's compare S, /S/ and Z, /Z/.

advice, advise
bounce, bounds
brace, braze
bus, buzz
hiss, his
peace, peas
price, prize
rice, rise
sag, zag
sap, zap
sink, zinc
sip, zip
sounds, zounds
Sue, zoo

If you're not sure of whether it should be pronounced as
S, /S/ or Z, /Z/, pronounce it as an S, /S/. You'll get away with
it most of the time.

Now let's practice S, /S/ and Z, /Z/ in sentences.

1. If you're satisfied, save the file and say good-bye.
2. Sing six songs and sail at sea then look at the sky to see if it's still sunny.
3. Sweep the dust on the glass and set it on the grass. It's a must.
4. Address our ambition before analyzing the bonus to our boss.
5. This practice is fabulous. Drink some juice then play chess on the bus.
6. If the alarm beeps, go straight to the ships.
7. Do zebras eat zucchinis? Absolutely!
8. Zigzag in the zombie zone. Zillion dollars is no use. This is no home.
9. Amazed! Citizens enjoying the blizzard with lizards.
10. If you can, bring a prize.
11. To maximize the prize, internationalize before you energize.
12. She finds her excuse with ease.
13. When the roaches approach the beaches, the feast finishes.

Again, if you're not sure of whether it should be pronounced as /S/ or /Z/, pronounce it as S, /S/.

Chapter 33: The /Y/ Sound

Let's hear the /Y/ sound.

Year, yes, yesterday, yet, unite, university, use, utility, crayon, onion

To pronounce the /Y/ sound, press the tip of our tongue against our lower front teeth, then raise the front part of our tongue and push the air out to produce the sound. /Y/. /Y/. /Y/.

Let's practice the /Y/ sound:

1. The /Y/ sound with the letter Y in front.
   yacht, yam, yard, yaw, year, yellow, yes, yesterday, yet, yield, Yo-yo, yogurt, yoke, young, youth, yummy

2. The /Y/ sound with the letter Y in the middle.
   beyond, coyote, crayon, kayak, lawyer, layout, loyal, mayo, mayor, payoff, player, Voyager

3. The /Y/ sound without the letter Y.
   amuse, beautiful, billion, computer, continue, contribute, curious, cute, Europe, excuse, fuel, fusion, future, huge, human, humid, January, menu, million, muse, museum, music, onion, pure, trial, unit, unite, university, use, value, view

Now let's practice /Y/ in sentences.

1. Yes, yesterday has gone away and tomorrow has yet to come. Utilize the current moment and use what you've got to play yo-yo.
2. How to make yummy yogurt? Ask Yager.
3. The mayor is loyal to the city. That's the payoff.
4. All football players are required to go to the tryout. They can bring a football or a papaya.
5. That's a cute menu. Did you bring it from Europe?
6. The fuel for the future will be hugely different. Good job, human!
7. This music is unique. Thanks a million.

Chapter 34: The /CH/ and the /J/ Sounds

Let's get familiar with the /CH/ sound.

achieve, archer, attachment, adventure, amateur, chair, chalk, chamber, digestion

To pronounce /CH/, slightly round our lips, press the tip of our tongue against our teeth to seal the gaps and build pressure, then quickly bring the tongue down to release the pressure to produce the /CH/ sound. /CH/. /CH/. /CH/.

Is /CH/ voiced or voiceless? /CH/ is voiceless. Let's practice /CH/:

1. When /CH/ is in the front.
   chain, chair, champion, chancellor, chant, chapter, charcoal, Charlie, chart, chase, chat, check, cheer, cheese, cheetah, cherry, chess, chew, chicken, chief, child, chin, chip, chore, chuck, chuckle, chunk

2. When /CH/ is in the middle.
   bachelor, benchmark, bleacher, catcher, enrichment, hitchhiker, ketchup, kitchen, luncheon, orchard, puncher, poncho, rancher, Richard, richer

3. When /CH/ is at the end.
   1. approach, attach, beach, brunch, bunch, catch, challenge, crunch, each, fetch, hatch, hitch, inch, itch, peach, perch, reach, rich, roach, stitch, such, switch, teach, touch, watch, which

4. The /CH/ sound formed from the letter T.
   adventure, amateur, culture, feature, fixture, future, mature, mixture, moisture, natural, nature, nurture, picture, posture, signature, structure, temperature, texture, combustion, exhaustion, question, suggestion

Now let's practice /CH/ in sentences.

1. The chancellor has changed. Started from the bottom of the food chain, he's now a champion.
2. Charlie was a chess player a year ago. He's now the chair of the chess department.
3. What's the fastest land animal on Earth, a cheetah or a chicken? When gliding from the sky, the cheetah will not fly, but the chicken will survive.
4. Richard got richer by hatching chickens in his orchard.
5. Approach the beach to find Peach is going to be a challenge.
6. Take an adventure of agriculture. If you're an amateur, enjoy the feature. Take a picture.
7. Add some moisture and some temperature to the structure and leave the rest to nature.
8. This is the combustion and this is the exhaustion. Any questions?

Now let's hear the /J/ sound.

jacket, Jacob, jewelry, gentleman, genuine, geography, encourage, energy, education

To pronounce /J/, slightly round our lips, touch our lower teeth with our tongue. Now push the air up from our belly. Add vibration. /J/. /J/. /J/.

Let's practice the /J/ sound.

1. The /J/ sound from the letter J.
    Jack, janitor, January, jar, jasmine, jaw, Jay, jeep, jelly, jet, jigsaw, jingle, join, joke, Joseph, journal, judge, juice, junior, just, adjective, adjust, conjunction, enjoy, major, majority, object, rejoice, subject

2. The /J/ sound from the letter G.
    gems, general, generate, generation, genius, geometry, gesture, giant, ginger, gym, age, agenda, agent, college, courage, engine, engineer, George, gyroscope, hinge, huge, knowledge, large, logical, manager, marriage, merge, orange, range, region, Virginia, wage

3. The /J/ sound from the letters DU.
    education, educator, gradual, graduate, graduation, individual, module, nodule, procedure, schedule

Now let's practice the /J/ sound in sentences.

1. Jack, the janitor, dropped his jaw when he saw Jasmine sleeping in her jar.
2. Jason and Jasmine enjoy joking about jelly in their jeep while journeying through the jungle.
3. Put the gel and gems together, then eat some ginger.
4. George is a giant. At the age of seven, he's huge in the region.
5. General Page is a genius. He's good at geometry and engineering.
6. Education will pay off. Follow the procedure until we graduate.

Now let's compare the /CH/ and /J/ sounds.

chain, Jane
charge, judge
cheep, jeep
cherry, Jerry
chill, Jill
choke, joke
choose, juice
chunk, junk
ranch, range
rich, ridge

Chapter 35: The /SH/ and the /ZH/ Sounds

Let's hear the /SH/ sound.

ship, shop, show, nation, option, magician, mission, tissue, immersion,

To pronounce /SH/, slightly close our teeth, round our lips and bring them forward. Roll our tongue and let the air flow out through our tongue. /SH/. /SH/. /SH/.

Is /SH/ voiced or voiceless?

Put a hand on our throat. /SH/. Do you feel any vibration?

Right. There is no vibration. /SH/ is voiceless.

Let's practice /SH/:

1. The /SH/ sound with SH.
    shadow, shampoo, shape, share, she, sheep, shepherd, shield, shift, shrimp, ash, astonish, brush, finish, fish, flash, flourish, fresh, lavish, marsh, push, vanish, wash

2. The /SH/ sound with the letters T and C.
    ambitious, collection, compulsion, emotion, fiction, information, initial, partial, patience, ratio, reaction, section, station, suction, ancient, associate, conscious, delicious, efficient, electrician, financial, gracious, Marcia, musician, ocean, Patricia, social, special

3. The /SH/ sound with the letters S and SS.
    dimension, extension, insurance, insure, mansion, Sean, sugar, sure, tension, assure, discussion, emission, impression, issue, permission, pressure

4. The /SH/ sound with the letters CH.

brochure, chalet, champagne, chandelier, chaperone, chef, chic, chute, machine, Michelle, mustache, parachute

Now let's practice /SH/ in sentences.

1. Shadow the shepherd to sheer the wool and shield the sheep from wolves.
2. Share the earth with shrimp, fish, sheep, and other animals.
3. Push the bush to finish the show then wash the marsh with ash.
4. Way to go! Our ambition is emotional.
5. This collection of information is ancient. Look at their reaction.
6. The electrician's financial situation is about the same as the magician and the musician. The difference is the musician likes the ocean.
7. What's the dimension of this mansion and the extension? I wonder how they pay for insurance.
8. This is the discussion of the emission. They have my impression and permission.
9. This is a brochure of the machine. You get a free parachute for being a chaperone, Michelle.

Now let's hear the /ZH/ sound.

composure, disclosure, camouflage, garage, massage

To pronounce the /ZH/ sound, round our lips and bring them forward. Roll our tongue and let the air flow out through our tongue.

/ZH/ sounds like /SH/, however, the /ZH/ sound is voiced. Place a hand on our throat. Feel the vibration before you move on. /ZH/. /ZH/. /ZH/.

The /ZH/ sound can be formed from the letters S, Z, and G. There are only a few words in English where the letter Z is pronounced as /ZH/.

Let's practice /ZH/.

1. The /ZH/ sound with the letters S and Z.
    azure, closure, enclosure, exposure, leisure,
    measure, pleasure, treasure, aversion, casual,
    conclusion, confusion, decision, delusion, fusion,
    infusion, occasion, persuasion, revision, television,
    transfusion, usual, version, vision, visual

2. The ZH sound with the letter G.
    beige, camouflage, collage, corsage, entourage,
    garage, genre, mirage, massage, prestige, regime

Let's practice /ZH/ in sentences.

1. Measure our pleasure with a ruler. What's the answer?
2. Find our treasure for leisure. Set the right exposure and take some pictures.
3. This casual conclusion is a good decision. If you have confusion, it's a delusion.
4. Highly successful people always have vision, decision, and occasionally confusion. Some of them have a television.
5. This beige cloth can stay camouflaged if it stays locked in our garage.

Now let's compare /SH/ and /ZH/.

assure, azure
fiction, vision
fuchsia, fusion
pressure, pleasure

Chapter 36: The TH Sounds

There are two different TH sounds. The voiced TH sound, /TH/, and the voiceless TH sound, /TH/.

Let's hear the voiceless TH sound, /TH/, first.

faith, health, math, thank, three, author, ether, ethics, birthday

To pronounce the voiceless TH sound, /TH/, slightly open our teeth and touch the lower front teeth with the tip of our tongue. While keeping the tip of our tongue there touching the lower front teeth, bring our tongue forward to touch our upper front teeth. /TH/, /TH/, /TH/.

Let's go over this again. To pronounce the voiceless TH sound, /TH/, slightly open our teeth and touch the lower front teeth with the tip of our tongue. Now keep the tip of our tongue there still touching our lower front teeth, bring the tongue forward to touch our upper front teeth. Therefore, the very tip of our tongue is now touching our lower front teeth, and a little bit above the tip of our tongue is now touching our upper front teeth.

Now that the very tip of our tongue is now touching our lower front teeth, and a little bit above the tip of our tongue is touching our upper front teeth, now push the air out and let the air flow out between our tongue and our teeth.

In other words, place the tip of our tongue between our front teeth as we produce the sound. Let me say this again, to produce the correct voiceless TH sound, the /TH/ sound, place the tip of our tongue between our front teeth as we push the air out and let the air flow out between the gaps between our teeth and our tongue.

All right. Now let's try these words again.

faith, health, math, thank, three, author, ether, ethics, birthday

To pronounce the voiceless TH sound, /TH/, where should we place the tip of our tongue? Between our front teeth! Place the very tip of our tongue behind our lower front teeth and a little bit above the very tip of our tongue between our front teeth.

Now let's get it.

1. The voiceless TH sound, /TH/, with TH in the beginning.
   thaw, theater, theme, theory, thermal, thesis, thick, thigh, thin, thing, think, third, thirsty, thirteen, thirty, thorough, thought, thousand, thrall, threat, three, threshold, thrifty, thrill, thrive, throat, throng, throughout, throw, thrust, thumb, thunder, Thursday

2. The voiceless TH sound, /TH/, with TH in the middle.
   Anthony, anthem, anthropology, anything, athlete, authority, bathroom, birthday, birthmark, Cathy, earthquake, ether, ethics, everything, faithful, healthy, lengthy, methane, method, monthly, python, something, synthetic, healthy, truthfulness, within, without, and again, birthday

3. The voiceless TH sound, /TH/, with TH at the end.
   bath, birth, cloth, booth, earth, faith, fourth, length, math, month, north, oath, path, sixteenth, Smith, smooth, south, stealth, wealth, with, worth, youth, zenith, warmth

Now let's practice the voiceless TH sound, /TH/, in sentences.

1. Thaw our frozen food in a thick thermal container for 33 minutes then go the theater in a theme park.
2. If you're the third thirstiest thrower, think three times before writing our thesis.
3. If you have thoroughly thought about thousands of theories, pick one that thrills you this Thursday.
4. Anthony has studied everything about anthropology except for birthday celebrations in the bathroom.
5. Arthur is a thin athlete who's six feet three but only 113 pounds.
6. Cathy tried to scrape her birthmark on her thigh during an earthquake and became faithful on healthy exercises.
7. Wrap a bath cloth for a month after birth then think about its worth.
8. On Earth, whether you want to go south or north, if you have faith, you can celebrate.

Before we move on to the voiced TH sound, /TH/, let's compare the voiceless TH sound, /TH/, with other similar sounds. The first one is the voiles TH sound.

thank, sank
thank, tank
thaw, saw
thaw, tall
theme, seam
theme, team
thick, sick
thick, tick
thigh, fi
thigh, sigh
thigh, tie
thin, fin
thin, sin
thin, tin
thing, ding
thing, sing
think, sink
third, cert
third, dirt
thirty, dirty
thorn, torn
thought, fought
thought, sought
thought, taught
thumb, dumb
thumb, sum
thumb, tum

How do we learn how to drive a car? By driving a car or by looking at how others drive a car? The answer is obvious. Just drive the car.

Now how do we learn how to say the voiceless TH sound right? By saying /TH/ or by listening to how others say /TH/? The answer is obvious. Just say /TH/. Here are more words with /TH/. Keep saying /TH/.

bath, bass
bath, bat
booth, boos
both, boat
both, Bose
eighth, ate
faith, face
fifth, fif
fifth, fit
fourth, force
Keith, keys
math, mass
math, mat
mouth, mouse
myth, miff
myth, miss
path, pat
Ruth, roof
sixth, six
teeth, teas
tenth, tent
tooth, to
truth, choose
with, whiff
with, whiz
with, wit
worth, worse

Now let's move on to the voiced TH, the /TH/ sound. Let's get familiar with the voiced TH, the /TH/ sound.

That, their, those, another, feather, rather.

To pronounce the voiced TH sound, /TH/, pronounce the voiceless TH sound, /TH/, then do the following two things:
1. Extend our tongue out a little more. Extend the area a little bit above the very tip of our tongue out.
2. Add vibration. /TH/.

Now, let's compare the voiceless TH sound, /TH/, with the voiced TH sound, /TH/.

/TH/, /TH/
/TH/, /TH/
/TH/, /TH/

1. Let's practice the voiced TH sound, /TH/, with TH in the beginning.
> than, that, the, thee, their, theirs, them, there, therefore, these, they, this, those, though, thus

Did you hear the vibration? /TH/? Good. We need that vibration!

2. Let's practice the voiced TH sound, /TH/, with TH in the middle.
> although, another, breathe, breather, brother, clothe, clothing, dither, either, farther, father, feather, further, gather, Heather, lather, leather, loathing, mother, neither, northern, other, rather, rhythm, seethe, slather, slither, smoother, smoothie, southern, teether, tether, together, weather, whether, wither

Did you say the TH sound with vibration? /TH/? Good. We need that vibration!

3. Now let's practice the voiced TH sound, /TH/, with TH at

the end.

There are none. If a word ends with TH, then TH is voiceless.

If you're not sure whether the TH in a word is voiced or voiceless, pronounce it as voiceless. We'll get away with it most of the time.

Let's practice the voiced TH, /TH/, in sentences.

1. That is their smoothie. Their smoothie is smoother than these.
2. Although they have brought their breather, they were unable to breathe when they walked. Therefore, they slithered.
3. Heather stayed with her father, mother, and brothers for another winter.
4. Gather our clothes, feather, and leather together, let's go farther.

Now let's compare the voiced TH sound, /TH/, with other similar sounds. The first one is the voiced TH sound.

Than, Dan
Than, tan
Than, fan
that, sat
that, tat
then, zen
then, den
then, ten
they, say
they, day
breathe, breath
clothe, cloth
dither, differ
clothing, closing
lather, latter
loathing, loading

The difference between the voiced TH and the voiceless TH is so little that native speakers often pronounce the voiced TH as the voiceless TH in casual speaking. If you're not sure of whether the TH in a word is voiced or voiceless, pronounce it as voiceless. You'll get away with it in casual conversation.

Chapter 37: The Roll Back Consonants

Congratulations! We have completed single consonants. Now let's try the following:

TCHDSPR.

In the above consonant cluster, there are six consonants together. How do we pronounce them? Let's put them in a sentence.

I wa**tched spr**ing thrived.

TCHDSPR. All six consonants are linked together.

Now let's take a look the following words.

latchstring
catchphrase
Archchronicler

These words have many consonants in a row. How do we pronounce them? Here is how to get them right:

Roll them back!

Start from the back then work our way backward.

Let's look at latchstring. Here is how to do it.
- ring
- tring
- string
- chstring
- tchstring
- latchstring

Look at catchphrase.

- rase
- phrase
- chphrase
- tchphrase
- catchphrase

Archchronicler.
- ler
- cler
- nicler
- ronicler
- chronicler
- chchronicler
- archchronicler

The key is to pronounce them from the back. Add another sound each time and keep adding. Start from the back. Yes, from the back!

Congratulations. These are the most difficult ones. Now let's do the easier ones.

Spring – ring, pring, spring
splash – lash, plash, splash
strong – rong, trong, strong
strive – rive, trive, strive

three – ree, three
through – rou, through
quick – wick, kwick
quest – west, kwest

blend – lend, blend
blue – lue, blue
dream – ream, dream
drink – rink, drink

Now we got the idea. How do we get them right? Roll them

back!

Chapter 38: The Dropped Consonants

In the vowels section, we've learned the dropped vowel sounds. Now let's look at the dropped consonant sounds.

When we pronounce the following words slowly, they sound original.

mountain, mitten, kitten, twenty, often, soften

However, in natural speaking, the T, /T/ sound in the middle of these words is dropped. Let's pronounce these words at a natural speed.

mountain, button, mitten, bitten, twenty, seventy, planting, wanted, often, soften

Now try to say the following words slowly.

Exactly, trusts, lists, clothes

In these words, some consonants are dropped even when saying them slowly. Instead of saying exacTly, drop the T and say exacly. Instead of saying lisTs, just say lis's. And look at this one – clothes.

Instead of saying cloTHez, just drop the TH and say cloz. It's pronunciation is "exactly" the same as close as in close the door.

Here are more.

compactly, confidently, contacts, contexts, Exactly, interacts, software, swiftly, texts

asked, masked, risked, tasked, tusked

attends, bonds, commands, Grand Central, Grandma,

kindness, profoundness

relentless, restless

clothes, lengths, months, moths, sloths, eighths, tenths, hundredths

West side, first trip, lost thought, stand still

Again, we intentionally drop some consonants to make our English sound more natural. Instead of saying

– asked,

say as'ed.

Instead of saying

– attends,

say attens.

The good news is, there are not too many of these. Memorize the words in this chapter, and as an ESL speaker, you'll have more than what you need to know.

Chapter 39: The Missing Consonants

Congratulations! We have finished learning consonants. Now when we learned vowel sounds in the first half of this lesson, you have missed the sounds of some consonants or mispronounced the sounds of some consonants.

Yes. You have!

Now let me say that again. When we learned vowels in the first half of this lesson, you have missed the sounds of some consonants or mispronounced the sounds of some consonants.

I have walked in your shoes before. I know you have. I know you have missed them or mispronounced them.

The good news is, now that we have learned consonants. Go back to the first half of the book and practice the vowel sounds. This time, get the consonants and get them right.

Go back there now. Go back there before we get to the next chapter.

Did I say go back to the beginning of the book now?

I guess I did say that. Let's go back to the beginning of the book now. Let's get those missing consonants and mispronounced consonants.

Do it all over again and then go to the next chapter.

Chapter 40: Liaison

Let's first look at the following two sentences. These two sentences are the same. However, the first one is the not-so-good way of saying the sentence. The second one is the good way of saying the same sentence.

The not-so-good way of saying it
    1. Today - is - the - best - time - to - practice - our - English.

Now the good way of saying it
    2. Today is the best time to practice our English.

Which one sounds better? Certainly the second one sounds better. The second one sounds way better! This is the right way to speak English. Let's listen to the second one again.
    2. Today is the best time to practice our English.

Let's compare the difference between the not-so-good way and the good way.
    Today is
    Today is
    Today is
    Today is

    Best time
    Best time
    Best time
    Best time

    Practice our
    Practice our
    Practice our
    Practice our

    Our English
    Our English

Our English
Ou<u>r E</u>nglish

The right way to speak English is to link the words together.

This is word liaison. It means word connection. When we speak English, we link words together in phrases and sentences.

Again, when we speak English, we link words together in phrases and sentences.

There are four ways to link words together.

1. Consonant to Consonant Liaison

Let's look at the following words.

Best time
Just talk
Help people
Top performance

These words end and begin with the same consonants. When we speak English, we link the two words together. As a result, "best time" becomes "bestime." "Just talk" becomes "justalk." Let's try them again.

Bes<u>t t</u>ime
Jus<u>t t</u>alk
Hel<u>p p</u>eople
To<u>p p</u>erformance

How do we link them together? Let's look. In "best time," we do the following:
   1. Extend the sound of /S/
   2. Drop the first T.

Bes*time.
Bes*time.
Bes*time.

Now let's try "just talk."
    3. Extend the sound of /S/
    4. Drop the first T.
Jus*talk.
Jus*talk.
Jus*talk.

Same thing for the "P" in "help people."
Hel*people.
Hel*people.
Hel*people.

For "top performance," extend the sound of O and drop the first P.
To*performance.
To*performance.
To*performance.

Now look at the following.
Good book
Lead team
Five forms
Self-victory
With them
Breathe through

In these words, the ending consonants are very similar to the beginning consonants, but they are not the same. Let's look at the first one.

Good book
/D/ and /B/ are very similar. We need to do two things.
    1. Reduce the sound of the first word "good" and
       increase the sound of the second word "book."

Goo**d book**
Goo**d book**
Goo**d book**

2. Cut the sound of the first word's ending consonant, the /D/ sound, into two halves, say the first half, and drop the second half. So, instead of saying goo/D/, just say goo/D/ by dropping the ending part of the /D/ sound. In other words, do not release the /D/ sound. However, it's not goo book. We need the say the first half of the /D/ sound. It's goo**d book**.

Goo**d book**
Goo**d book**
Goo**d book**

Now let's look at breath**e th**rough.
The TH in breathe is voiced, /<u>TH</u>/, but the TH in through is voiceless, /TH/. This is what we need to do:

1. Reduce the sound of the first word "breathe" and increase the sound of the last word "through."

Breath**e th**rough
Breath**e th**rough
Breath**e th**rough

2. Cut the sound of the first TH into two halves, say the first half, drop the second half, and then link to the next TH sound. In other words, put your teeth and tongue in the correct position, do not release the sound of the first TH, but release the sound of the second TH.

Breath**e th**rough
Breath**e th**rough
Breath**e th**rough

Now you got the idea. Let's try them again.
Goo**d book**
Lea**d team**
Fiv**e forms**
Sel**f-v**ictory
Wi**th them**
Breath**e th**rough

2. Consonant to Vowel Liaison

Let's go one step deeper. Take a look at the following words.
Like it
Hold on
Put up
Strong enough

The first words can perfectly connect to the next word. As they connect, they form a new sound.
Li<u>ke i</u>t
Hol<u>d o</u>n
Pu<u>t up</u>
Stro<u>ng e</u>nough

Let's try them again.
Li<u>ke i</u>t
Hol<u>d o</u>n
Pu<u>t up</u>
Stro<u>ng e</u>nough

Get them right. Let's practice.
Tell a story. Tel<u>l a</u> story.
Have a good day. Ha<u>ve a</u> goo<u>d d</u>ay.
Eight o'clock. Eigh<u>t o</u>'clock.
Wait till eleven. Wai<u>t ti</u><u>ll e</u>leven.

3. Vowel to Vowel Liaison

Let's look at the phrase "he is."
When we say it separately, it's "he - is."
When we say it with connection, it's "h<u>e i</u>s."
H<u>e i</u>s

H**e i**s

Do you hear an extract /Y/ sound between he and is?
H**e i**s
H**e i**s

Yes. There is an extract /Y/ sound between the words. Let's try more.
Sh**e i**s
Jerr**y u**nderstands
I **a**m
B**y a**ir
The**y a**sked
St**ay o**n
The b**oy a**pplied
Enj**oy a** vacation

The good news is, the /Y/ sound is automatically generated. Let's try them again.
Sh**e i**s
Jerr**y u**nderstands
I **a**m
B**y a**ir
The**y a**sked
St**ay o**n
The b**oy a**pplied
Enj**oy a** vacation

Right! The /Y/ sound is automatically generated. That is because our mouth is already in the correct position when we say a word that ends with an /E/ ending sound. Words with the /E/ ending sounds are words with /E/, /I/, /A/, and /OY/ endings.

Let's practice more.
I **a**ls**o i**nvited th**e o**ther team.
Thr**ee o**ther teams part**y u**nder th**e u**mbrella.
I **u**nzipped th**e a**irbag.

Congratulations! Since the /Y/ sound is automatically generated, we only need to understand it and that's all.

Now let's understand one more. Again, let's learn it by practicing it.

> G<u>o o</u>n
> G<u>o o</u>n

Do you hear an extract /W/ sound between go and on?

> G<u>o o</u>n
> G<u>o o</u>n

Yes. There is an extract /W/ sound between the words. Let's try more.

> Joe is
> Row 18
> How about
> Allow it
> Who is
> You excel

Same thing! The /W/ sound is automatically generated. That is because our mouth is already in the correct position when we say a word that ends with an /O/, /OO/, and /OW/ ending sounds.

Let's practice more.

> G<u>o o</u>n t<u>o A</u>ven<u>ue A</u>.
> Contin<u>ue e</u>ight more days.
> Wh<u>o is</u> sitting on R<u>ow 18</u>?
> Y<u>ou e</u>xcel when y<u>ou a</u>pply.

Congratulations! Since the /W/ sound is automatically generated, we only need to understand it and that's all.

4. Consonant to Y Liaisons

4.1. First, let's look at the T to Y liaison:

Wha**t y**ou need is practice.
Ac**t y**our part.
Don'**t y**ou like it?
I go**t y**ou.

As T and Y link together, they naturally form a CH sound.

What **y**ou → Wha**ch**oo
Ac**t y**our → Ac**ch**oor
Don'**t y**ou → Don**ch**oo
Go**t y**ou → Got**ch**oo

4.2. Let's look at the D to Y liaison:

Di**d y**ou see that?
Woul**d y**ou like one?
How di**d y**esterday go?
I plan to atten**d Y**elena's party.

As D and Y link together, they naturally form a J sound.

Di**d y**ou → Did**j**a
Woul**d y**ou → Wü**j**oo
Di**d y**esterday → Did**j**esterday
Atten**d Y**elena's → Attend**j**elena's

4.3. Now the S and Y liaison:

That sound**s yummy**.
Si**x y**ears.
Deliciou**s y**ams

Note that "six" is pronounced as "siks." The last letter as it sounds is /S/. As /S/ and Y connect, they form a SH sound.

Sound'**s y**ummy → Sound**sh**ummy

Si**x** **y**ears → Sik**sh**ears
Deliciou**s** **y**ams → Deliciou**sh**ams

4.4. Now the last one, the Z and Y liaison:

Sei**z**e **y**our sword.
Reali**z**e **y**our potential.
Murphy**'s** **y**ams.

Note that the "S" in "Murphy's" is pronounced as /Z/. As /Z/ and Y connect, they form a ZH sound.

Sei**z**e **y**our sword → Sei**zh**oors sword.
Reali**z**e **y**our potential → Reali**zh**oors potential.
Murphy**'s** **y**ams → Murphy**zh**ams.

Chapter 41: To Our Journey!

Congratulations! We have learned English pronunciation!

Did you record your practices? If you haven't, do it. You'll be proud of your progress! Compare the very first one with the very last one. How was your pronunciation before? How is it now?

Now look at this. My name is Ken Xiao. I didn't speak any English when I moved to America at the age of 17, but listen to my English now. You're listening to my voice.

How did I do that? I even wrote a book on how I did it. The book is called *Talk English*.

Use the steps in Chapter 2. Practice again and again, and we will get our English pronunciation 100% correct!

To our journey,

Ken Xiao

Other books by Ken Xiao

CPSIA information can be obtained
at www.ICGtesting.com
Printed in the USA
FSHW021527030920
73544FS

9 780998 163291